D0970436

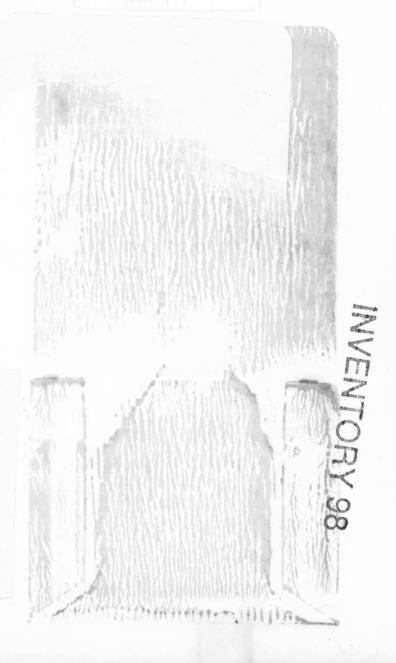

The Theatre Crafts Book of Costumes

Edited and with
an introduction by

C. Ray Smith

THEATRE CRAFTS BOOKS
RODALE PRESS, INC. EMMAUS, PA. 18049

Table of Contents

3

Introduction

by C. Ray Smith

Most costume books tell us what people wore in different periods, or how to drape a toga, fold a wimple, shirr a ruff, build a bustle. Most costume books are histories of clothes throughout the ages, or guides to recreating period dress. This book is an exception.

"The Theatre Crafts Book of Costume" is about the work of practicing costume designers in today's theatre. It presents their ideas, their passion and dedication, their methods, their approaches to the history of clothes as well as a boon of practical insights into their craft. "The Theatre Crafts Book of Costume" tells how today's designers decide, in the first place, whether or not to design a toga, wimple, ruff, or bustle, then, if they choose to, how they go about it.

As often as not, however, a costumer's work goes unnoticed in the theatre. It is overlooked— seen but not seen. Theatregoers see the figures on the stage; often they rave ecstatically about the settings. Less often do they recognize the significant contributions of the costumes. Almost never do they see the significance or subtle characterization of modern dress costumes. Nor are laymen the only theatregoers guilty of this negligence; many professional theatre people are costume-blind—including most professional theatre critics. This book aims to reverse that neglect. "The Theatre Crafts Book of Costume" speaks not only to costume designers but to all lovers of the theatre and the performing arts. It speaks about the unsuspectedly rich layers of interest that costume design has for all theatregoers.

In the singular craft of costume design, we have a detailed yet overall view of contemporary theatre. As this volume reveals, costume design can show us the spectrum of our theatrical productions; it reveals the variety of producing organizations and the diversity of professional costume designers. Like the other backstage crafts, costume design illustrates in microcosm the processes and practices of the great amalgam that constitutes theatre.

For performers' costumes are more than clothes, more than high fashion clothes, more even than the history of high fashion clothes. In the theatre, as in portrait painting, clothes give the picture form, color, line, and texture, but primarily they establish the fundamental character of the portrait. Stage pictures are full-scale, living portraits. Again as in portrait painting, costume takes precedence over scenic background in indicating character. Whereas set designers fill in the background, costume designers work on the portrait itself.

As in the fine art of painting, two mainstreams of design also exist in contemporary theatre costumes: on the one hand we have abstract design, and on the other, representational or realistic design. These two directions lead to all the theatre

6

images we create today—historical reconstructions, contemporary actualizations, or futuristic visions. That each costume designer must make this basic choice for each production tells us the dimensions of his work.

Costume designers who work in the representational mode aim for period accuracy in clothing design. Yet they focus, ultimately, on the goal of portraying true and telling characterizations for each individual performer. Whether in costumes from earlier eras or in modern dress, accurate representation must add directional signals—signposts, as it were—that point to the characters of those portrayed on stage—even including the out-of-datedness of certain seedy characters. Today's interest in this representational approach is a fuller development of the 19th Century historical revival and that century's passion for exact reconstruction; it also indicates how devoted we are today to reviving plays from other ages—how devoted we are to 20th Century historical revival.

The second approach—abstract design—leads to ambiguous, dehumanized forms or to stylizations based more on convention than on character. Abstract costumes are common to modern dance and to ballet as well as to 20th Century dramas written at the time of early abstraction in the fine arts. Stylized costumes, which are traditional in the circus, in ice shows, in children's theatre, and elsewhere also tend toward abstraction. Even they reveal character, but they do so at a larger scale than representational costumes do: Abstract costuming provides the basic character of the overall stage picture.

The costume designers whose work is discussed in this volume proclaim their partnership in the theatre with a heartwarming sense of dedication. They continually demonstrate loving care for every aspect of their crafts. Eye-opening is their meticulous attention to the minutest detail of specialization — color, line, texture, materials, handcraft workmanship, aging of fabrics. Even when a costume designer is functioning primarily as a shopper — at a couturier's or a costume rental firm — the full process of his craft seems enthusiastically called into play.

The professional costume designers represented in this volume are diverse enough to present a wide survey of current costume design practices. They speak of differences in emphasis at regional and repertory theatres, at Broadway and Off-Broadway theatres, at the ballet, circus, and opera, in educational and environmental theatre. The productions they discuss range from classic to contemporary to avant-garde, from realistic to futuristic, from sober to joyous, from silly to relevant. Together they illuminate, through the vision of costume design, the rich fabric of today's theatre.

This survey of procedures covers the research and design phase, the production phase, and the business practices of costume designers. Both representational and abstract research and design are described. Alwin Nikolais tells of his formless, amoebic costumes for ballet; Douglas A. Russell recalls his abstract, geologic inspirations for Greek drama. Several essays outline imaginative procedures for selecting a historical period and a tone for costumes. William D. Roberts and Kurt Wilhelm contrast two different visions of the same Moliere play; Patton Campbell takes us through his consistent design process for two different productions. Recreation of a selected period with both historical accuracy and quality of character occupies a number of costume designers, as Theoni Aldredge, Jane Greenwood, and Peter Harvey de-

8

scribe. Also, in the research and design phase, Nancy Potts reminds us that a costume designer must visualize color and line in flow, in movement, and not merely as they appear in static design sketches.

In the subsequent production and maintenance phases, Theoni Aldredge stresses a designer's concern for ensuring that costumes are finished by the appointed time. Nancy Potts and Leo Van Witsen plead for costumes that are durable — for the length of a run, or several seasons of repertory. And Peter Harvey adds that a successful play that runs a long time and fosters additional performing companies can also foster a frustrating predicament for its costume designer, that is, how to reorder a fabric for a costume several years later when the fabric has gone out of stock.

Among the business practices that costume designers show concern for, open and honest communication among all the members of the producer's team is strongly endorsed by several. Budgets are passionate concerns of Leo Van Witsen and all those in environmental and children's theatre. Several designers make comparisons with the economics of costume design in Europe.

9

Fortunately, all these designers have devised valuable solutions to specific production, maintenance, and business problems that will aid students as well as intrigue professional colleagues. "Theatre Crafts" is grateful to them for helping to make known their design procedures and the preoccupations of today's costume designers. It is a richly informative, rather charming and winning portrait of costume design, bringing to light, the character of a theatre craft that is largely seen but not often praised for all its glory.

Theoni Aldredge's troll costumes for "Peer Gynt" were so effective that Walter Kerr recommended they be sent to the Smithsonian Institution.

Passionate dedication to the quality of costume designing is the keynote of Theoni Aldredge's infectious plea about budgets. Her concern for careful communication between members of the collaborating design team aims zealously at both quality of design and at producing finished costumes with an unwavering eye on the schedule. Her own work evokes the "wonder and awe" that she feels for the theatre, and her credits inspire similar admiration.

Theoni Aldredge is the resident designer for the New York Shakespeare Festival; she has created costumes for the Festival's productions of "Much Ado," "King Lear," "A Midsummer Night's Dream," "Hamlet," "Othello," and thirty others. On Broadway she has designed costumes for "The Best Man," "The Devil's Advocate," "I Can Get It For You Wholesale," "Who's Afraid of Virginia Woolf," "Any Wednesday," "Cactus Flower," "You Know I Can't Hear You When the Water's Running," and "Illya Darling." Her film designs include: "No Way to Treat A Lady," "Last Summer," and "You're A Big Boy Now."

The following article was first published in "Theatre Crafts" magazine in November/December, 1969.

Costumes and the Budget

by Theoni V. Aldredge

Constantly we are reminded of the high cost of theatre. But what does that have to do with artistic integrity? Or is it because of the high cost that we feel all the anguish, fear, and panic? If so, is the theatre now becoming just another business? Has it come to the point where all we discuss, all we are concerned with, is the cost of things? There used to be a time when we talked about a show in terms of how many acts it would have. Now we talk about the "BUDGET," and because of this something very vital, very necessary has gone out of the theatre.

There was a time when the director and the artists he chose to work with would sit together for days and discuss a show with love and understanding, while respecting each other's talents. Points of view were tossed around, and movement, character, shape, and color were discussed. Everyone was allowed to contribute; everyone was allowed to agree and disagree. It was not a question of pleasing one or a hundred people. It was a question of pleasing each other. Each had a responsibility, and each treasured that responsibility. We did not always agree; we argued a lot, because we all wanted to give our best. It was during those discussions that we learned and grew.

Now budget is the primary concern. A designer will take his sketches to the costume shop, and the costume shop will give the producer a price. The next thing the designer hears from the producer is that the costumes are too expensive — where can we cut? So, the designer goes over his sketches again and again and starts cutting. Off comes the flower on that hat, or the ruffle on a petticoat, and the long fringe on the shawl. By doing this cutting, sometimes we take off anywhere from two hundred to a thousand dollars depending on the size of the show.

But every time I have been asked to cut on the budget, the show looked it. Somehow it never seems to be right. One can always do it for less, particularly if he doesn't care — but I care.

No Communication

This emphasis on budgetary concerns has brought about a new problem for designers. In recent years the costume designer has been told pretty much what is needed in a show, where to have the costumes built, and how to do them. Consequently, his responsibility is merely delivering a show on time — just exactly as he had been asked to do. There is no longer the kind of communication among members of a show that produces the most successful results.

How many times the curtain goes up on a show that I have designed and I don't recognize it as mine!

What happened to the original sketches between the day they went into the costume shop and the opening night in New York? What is that yellow dress doing on the stage? What happened to that lovely lavender one? The

14

In "Peer Gynt" the Ladies of Lust costumes give a designer challenge and inspiration, as sketches by Theoni Aldredge show (pp. 15 & 16).

answer is that, well, the scene did not work with the actress wearing the lavender dress. The sad thing is that they all worked on the dress instead of on the scene, and in the long run the scene did not work, not even with a yellow dress.

Extraordinary things happen during out of town tryouts, where anything can be changed from a shoe lace to a flower on an actress' lapel because somebody's wife, aunt, uncle, someone's artistic child, or even a secretary thought it should be changed.

I am not saying that designers are always right, but I like to be informed if I have done a bad job. The only way I'll ever know is to be allowed to look at my bad job and my mistakes, not somebody else's. What I object to is the interference of people who know nothing about costumes and much less about theatre, in addition to the people who listen to them, who should know about costumes and about theatre.

So where does it go wrong? One is told there is no room for mistakes in the theatre — nonsense! We are not dealing with either gods or superhumans. We are dealing with people; therefore, we are going to make mistakes. All we can hope and try for is not to make the same ones twice.

My Work

Let me give a few examples from my recent work. Where and how do you start designing for the musical version of "Billy Budd"? It must look real and yet that reality has to work on a musical stage. How much can you take out of the period book of the late 19th Century, and how much can you contribute as a designer? When will that magic moment come where reality stops and theatre comes in. What does the show say? What should it look like? Discussing all these things with the director, the choreographer, the scenic designer, and the lighting designer is always the most exciting part of a show for me. With "Billy Budd," we all arrived at a style, and we were happy. We all strive for something new and exciting. Sometimes we succeed; sometimes we fail. "Billy Budd" failed, and it hurt because we all hoped for so much and tried so hard.

17

Where was the magic we all hoped for? I don't know, but I intend to keep looking for it.

My work for the New York Shakespeare Festival in the summer 1969 production of "Peer Gynt" shows how different designing can be. It was a pleasure to work with producer Joseph Papp, who was not primarily concerned with costume budget cuts. The end result was so successful that Walter Kerr of "The New York Times" was able to suggest that my troll costumes should be sent to the Smithsonian Institution.

Theatre is a most complicated piece of machinery. It is a place of awe and wonder—a place where a group of dedicated artists work together and create together, a place where there must be constant communication among everyone involved. It is a place where—in order to be successful—everybody's contribution is not only necessary but vital.

The wonder of the theatre is that every good experience has a marvelous way of erasing the bad ones. A producer once told me that actors don't know the difference about a costume anyway, and that, after all, they are a dime a dozen. I disagree on both counts. I find it difficult to imagine theatre without producers—or without directors and designers. But I find it impossible to imagine theatre without actors—or costumes.

19

Sketch for Billy Budd.

The American theatre's seemingly elusive goal — repertory — is also its dream of an incomparable training ground. There, in a hothouse garden, prized posies grow distinct and sometimes thorny beauty. A designer must provide the tender craft of careful consideration, communication, and cooperation if his costume blossoms are to flourish. In addition, the frequency of actor changes within a role reduplicates the problem of costume changes, as Nancy Potts more minutely elaborates, and at a maintenance level, the personnel changes among dressers are often at war with the durability of the costumes. But the repetition of resolving these design situations is what makes a costumer's craft grow.

In the following article, first published in "Theatre Crafts" in July/August 1967, Nancy Potts writes of her experience with the APA/Phoenix Repertory Company, where she designed many successful productions, including "School for Scandal," "Show Off," and "Pantagleize." She started designing on her own at the age of sixteen, attended Washington University, and then served a period designing fashions for some well-known Seventh Avenue clothes houses. She has produced the costumes for 35 Broadway and Off-Broadway productions and twice received Tony Award nominations. She supervised the painting and aging of the costumes in the musical "Fiddler on the Roof," for which she won a

*Tony award. Her costumes for "Panta-
gleize" earned the Maharam Distinguished
Design Award and the Saturday Review
Best Costume Award. Her costumes for
"Hair" received the Theatre Yearbook
Award. In the 1971–72 season, she designed
the costumes for the musical version of
Truman Capote's "The Grass Harp," which
opened the University of Michigan's Power
Center and then moved to Broadway.*

Costumes for a Repertory Theatre

by Nancy Potts

21

No other design process in the theatre involves as much daily dependency upon the personalities, the foibles, the idiosyncrasies, and the sixth senses of the performer as does costume design. Because of this, it would be difficult to divorce my own wants and needs from my work. And so, had I refused to work within the limitations that a reper-tory theatre presents, as so many designers have, I would not have had the opportunity to grow, to know that style is not contingent upon money, or to appreciate satisfaction in terms of contributions to a play and company.

For the APA/Phoenix Repertory Company Nancy Potts designed "The School for Scandal" starring Helen Hayes as Mrs. Candor, Rosemary Harris as Lady Teazel, and Dee Victor as Lady Sneerwell (above).

For me, repertory theatre is a constant extension of myself as both a person and a costume designer. Because it is not a transitory, performance-to-performance association of theatre people but a continuing inter-relationship, everyone learns what such things as compromise really means. It is not a giving in or the artistic sacrifice everyone fears. Instead, it is learning to listen and to communicate. For instance, I will never change one detail in a costume until I have been given the opportunity to say why I designed it as I did. It leads to a great expansion because you know full well that any one of hundreds of costumes will work for a particular character. Refining reasons why a particular costume will or will not work is simply a matter of a point of view.

In a one-shot show situation, every actor is concerned primarily with how he looks in his costume. And with a strong personality or a star, certain deferences must be paid. Yet, in a repertory situation this problem is lessened because everyone's attitude is toward the complete concept of the play. Although there is the usual eruption of temperament and the self-indulgence, there also is the knowledge that we will be working with each other again and again. Eventually, the areas of compromise become smaller and smaller.

Axioms of Repertory

Anyone working in a repertory theatre immediately becomes aware of two facts. If the object of a design or the design for a number of shows is primarily to show off the designer—for his own personal aggrandizement—he will not last long in a repertory set-up. The play—the collective concept—is of primary importance and it is toward this all of us work.

Secondly, there is no one way any particular play must be done. That is, there is no definitive production of anything.

My costumes, therefore, should always be meaningful to the play and to the concepts of the play. For me to superimpose a style, which may be diametrically opposed to it, would be defeating the very idea of a repertory theatre.

This resolves itself by working with the same company and it affords me an opportunity to have a better idea of what I can do with a particular costume since I know all about the actor who will be wearing it. I know what he will need in terms of adjustment, how well he wears certain colors, and so on. It's a big difference from the usual situation.

23

Many times a show is designed before it is fully cast. So concepts may change according to whomever is cast. (Sometimes the change is major, other times slight—nevertheless there are changes.) Wonderful concepts between designer and director go by the boards because certain performers cannot wear (or a star will not wear) certain costumes.

Basically then, how well I have designed my costumes to complement the entire production is the final evaluation of my work. Not individual designs.

So many designers have found an easy way out in their designs of period plays, especially by slavishly adhering to the line and detail of the particular period. They simply reproduce a silhouette (or the combinations of several silhouettes) they happen to find in a source book. Because their costumes are historically correct, the designer assumes they cannot be wrong for the production. This method or interest in single costumes can prove troublesome and lead to inaccuracies. It can, in effect, neglect to make statements about characters in the play. Period styles must be relevant to what the costumes themselves say about the character, what the costume states about the particular character in comparison with the other characters, and what the particular status of the character is, not only in the historical period but also in the play. All of these factors must be accounted for.

For example, within the framework of a 17th century society, there were some very specific reasons why certain articles of clothing were worn that certainly could be used as a means of identifying the type of person wearing them. If the hero were a cavalier, for instance (and during the time of the play's setting cavaliers were bedecked with ribbons), the impact of this exact costume might convey a dandy rather than a man of heroic stature. Clothes can convey no significance, or the wrong significance, to today's audiences.

So, rather than design costumes singly, I decide first where I want the design of the play to go. This almost automatically divides my costume approach into blocks or a series of subdivisions. Women of certain social *strata* might make up one block, the antagonists of royalty another, the antagonists of a lower social level another, and so on. Now I have a number of costume units that must go in a specific direction. The heads of the households among the antagonists of royal blood, women in the court but of great influence to the direction of the play, are the types of sub-divisions I make up. Each of these units can be divided further without ever losing an interdependency.

Once I have decided on my blocks, I work with color or rather a lack of it. Actually there isn't a color that cannot be reduced to a neutral without still expressing a value. And although it depends on the play, I have a tendency to

Nancy Potts' sketches for Signora Sirelli in Pirandello's "Right You Are If You Think You Are" (above left), and for Lady Teazle in Sheridan's "School For Scandal" (above right).

remain among the neutrals. Interestingly enough, the plays we have done at APA haven't lent themselves to a great deal of color.

After working color values to my satisfaction, I return to my concept of the play and determine the line. Certain elements of the line will be established by the period, so when I begin looking at my concept in its entirety, it is important to know how I will handle and balance color.

The line or style of the costumes will be a unifying factor for my design, but the variations I pick or eliminate within the line will reinforce the character. For instance, a particular braid may be an essential detail for a costume of a particular period, but if I felt it wouldn't work I would eliminate it without hesitation.

The Effects of Detail

When working with costume detail, practical considerations become major deciding factors. Specifically, I keep in mind the kind of house I am designing for. Naturally, in a small house details are more important and meaningful. But so many carefully chosen details that look great in a dressing-room mirror disappear completely on a larger house's stage. I always design for the middle of the house where the play will be produced.

A trick of looking at costumes from the wrong end of a telescope helps me keep my balance for details and fabric. That is, I simply mentally reverse a telescope and imagine how a costume will look reduced in size. It is interesting to try, since details that seemed so vital suddenly wash away. It is sometimes so difficult to remember that it doesn't count what a costume looks like up close — it's what it looks like from the house that matters.

And yet it is in the making of the costumes — the building of them — that the final results rest. Dependency upon a sketch is risky and dangerous. An audience doesn't see a sketch — a flat two-dimensional picture with flat color. Rather the audience sees a moving, three-dimensional flow of fabric and color. This is what should be behind each sketch and ultimately in the mind's eye of the designer.

For me a sketch supplies the mood, the sweep of a costume. But once in the workroom, the design process starts

*Costume sketches for a typical male character (above left) and for
Lady Sneerwell (above right) in "School for Scandal."*

all over again, transferring the mood and sweep of the sketch into fabric. I can faithfully reproduce a sketch, but it may not have anything to do with anybody else's interpretation of a faithful reproduction. Or, I can have the sketch duplicated and sent out to ten different shops, sit back and get ten incredibly different costumes.

Choosing Fabrics

Many times fabrics must be dyed specially or printed specially because of the demands of certain periods. Each step is, of course, a decision, always bearing in mind that what the audience sees and assumes is not necessarily what actually is on stage. Whether it would be easier and less expensive to order fabric or fake it is a major consideration.

With fabrics chosen, color and line established, I begin building my costumes. At APA this is a specialty all in itself because each role is double and sometimes triple cast. This, of course, means several different approaches that would be used for a one-shot show. *One* costume cannot be built for the two or three performers playing the role nor can the same pattern be used. Sizes and proportions change the cutting and pattern.

Often the style of the original costume may not fit the alternate performer at all and subsequently a new costume may have to be designed, approved, and built. This cannot be a haphazard design, of course, since it must fit into the concept.

28

Each alternate's costume is built as I build the original costume and, since we have large cast shows, time is a major factor. Ideally we should have a four-week workroom time schedule.

Administration is the biggest problem, especially for the wardrobe-master. He has costumes for nine shows to account for at all times and, because the shows are constantly changing, his headaches are compounded. Dressers must be trained and become adept at knowing what costumes the actors they are responsible for will need — and when. We spend more money on this phase than in building the costumes. Because of the constant shuffling and reshuffling of costumes, and because of the extraordinary number of pressings and cleanings they are subjected to, they must be built especially well. Material and workmanship cannot be sacrificed.

Without technical know-how, the best-intended concept can disintegrate and the most ideal costume would not last beyond a single wearing. Arriving at a sketch everyone agrees upon is the 10% inspiration; the other 90% is the perspiration that is needed to get that 10% into the costume for any modicum of success.

James Edmund Brady presents a solid basic survey of another regional theatre costume designer's methods in choosing period silhouettes, colors, and fabrics and also in dyeing, cutting, sewing, hemming, and finishing. In addition, he discusses shoes, handbags, hats, gloves, and jewelry as well as the procedure of shopping for costumes.

After graduating from the Maryland Institute College of Art, Brady studied costume design at the Bristol Old Vic Theatre School and designed costumes for the Bristol Old Vic's productions of "Volpone," "The Heiress," "The Crucible," "Yerma," "The York Cycle of Mystery Plays," and "Edward II." In Baltimore he designed for the Peabody Opera Company, the Baltimore City Ballet, and for Center Stage, where he was resident designer when the following article was published in "Theatre Crafts," March/April 1969. Since then he has designed for the Olney Theatre in Maryland, the Actors Theatre in Louisville, the Rep Theatre at the Loretto Hilton Center in St. Louis, and for Long Wharf Theatre's "You Can't Take It With You," which was presented at the Edinburgh Festival in 1971. He has most recently designed costumes for "The English Mystery Plays," "Measure for Measure," "The Journey of the Fifth Horse," and "Cat Among the Pigeons" at the Milwaukee Repertory Theatre Company.

Designing for
Regional Theatre

by James Edmund Brady

Designing for regional theatre can be one of the most stimulating yet taxing jobs for a young costume designer. Productions run the gamut of every period and style imaginable; working conditions can be horrendous and obstacles, multiple. For example, no sooner is a 1605 production of "Hamlet" on the boards than a 1927 production of "The Royal Family" is in the making. As a proving ground for designers, regional theatre is ideal.

At Baltimore's Center Stage, detail, scale, and color relations form a triumvirate that governs the designer's work. The 320-seat theatre has a three-quarter thrust stage, with a main acting area of 16 feet by 16 feet, and an overhanging balcony and stair units. Consequently, the designer must constantly hold in check any inclination toward over-elaboration. And since the audience is close enough to the stage to notice every stitch, his costumes must be as perfectly detailed as ordinary clothes, yet as durable as combat uniforms.

Vintage 1927 with a combination of the conservative and the theatrical was the basic approach for Baltimore's Center Stage production of "The Royal Family,"

"The Royal Family," written by George S. Kaufman and Edna Ferber, was first produced in 1927. Douglas Seale, Artistic Director of Center Stage, decided to maintain that period. The play, since it deals with universal human foibles, is not dated. And although the characters are caught up in a comical situation, they are concrete, real people, and their clothes must be as real as possible.

After reading the script, I was a bit stunned to realize that although I was well acquainted with the silhouette of the '20's, when it came to applying it to this play I drew a complete blank. As every designer knows, some of the clothes of the '20's were very unflattering—in fact, terrible. Yet one of the most important aspects of costume design is to flatter the players. When a style is chosen, the designer, without losing his total concept, must keep in mind the company that will wear it. Actors and actresses cannot go on stage feeling freakish; they must feel completely comfortable in the garments they wear. No good will come of sending someone on stage in a costume that, although absolutely accurate, makes him feel uncomfortable and self-conscious. It would jeopardize his performance, and no production is worth that!

Research for the Cavendishes

The designer must also make allowances for the change in silhouette. For example, compare the normal body line of today's woman with the elongated, flat-chested fashion mannequin of the '20's. Therefore, I began my research for "The Royal Family" by searching for pictures and descriptions of the underpinnings of the '20's. For this is where costumes begin—before fabrics are selected, before colors and accessories are chosen. The change in silhouette also applies to the men. Today, men's clothes are molded to their frames, whereas in the '20's they were a great deal fuller.

I wanted the Cavendishes—the Royal Family of Broadway—to project all the intimate realism, the life, of people in an old photograph album. The rotogravure section of the newspapers and the fashion magazines of the period gave me a good indication of what the family might have worn. But pinpointing what they would actually wear in the play was a difficult process.

33

My first set of drawings was terribly theatrical and very flamboyant. But after thinking about it, I felt this silhouette did not sit right. The characters in the play had reached a certain plateau. Julie is a successful actress; her mother, Fanny, is the great lady of the stage of a bygone era; and Julie's daughter, Gwenn, is being rushed by the Smart Set. And then there is Tony, who, as his mother says, is constantly getting himself into the tabloids for his playboy behavior.

Portraying these people as gypsies was clearly not the answer. So back to the drawing board I went, discarding many of my original ideas. I put myself in the place of the Cavendishes and came up with a look that combines a touch of the conservative with a touch of the theatrical.

A real problem arose in the designs for Fanny. What would a great trouper wear in her retirement? The play states that in each act Fanny appears in a tea gown. However, I wanted to convey the feeling that these gowns were not of the period of the play itself but 15 or 20 years earlier. So my research took me back to the turn of the century, to afternoon dresses. They gave me the silhouette I finally chose for Fanny—very soft, very feminine, perhaps a touch theatrical. Fanny was set at last and I started the final renderings.

The costumes for the rest of the characters evolved in the same way: after redoing the drawings, changing ideas around, I established final silhouettes, then submitted finished renderings.

34 The next step was to work out the color plot and the direction in which I wanted the colors to go. At the end of the play Fanny dies on stage and I felt all the colors should focus toward this climax. Taking my cue from the play itself: "Fanny dies in plum," I worked backwards, starting with dark shades and working toward light. In other words, I started my color scheme at the end of the play and worked forward to the beginning.

Then the real work began. How were these things to go together? The dresses would be cut on the bias. But not everything hangs well on the bias-cut, so I had to be careful of what materials I used: in the suits, for example, I substituted a very lightweight flannel for heavy wool,

A tea gown for Fanny (above) in "The Royal Family" was designed by James Edmund Brady as if it were 15 to 20 years earlier than the 1927 setting of the play.

which would not have draped properly. Some of my materials were difficult to get. For one costume I wanted a satin-backed crepe with a lot of silk in it. This sounds like a simple request, but it's worth your life to find it.

I feel it is extremely important to use the proper kind of fabrics on stage, not simply because our audience is so close but because good fabrics light and move better.

When all the fabrics had been collected I had to start compromising on color. Most of the colors I selected were three or four shades lighter than those I had conceived because I knew I would have to do a lot of re-dying anyhow to get the precise tones in my renderings.

This is the point where regional theatre becomes horrendous—when there are only two washing machines in which to dye an entire show. Sometimes it presents a comic situation, other times a tragic one. I wanted a certain shade of French gray for Julie's first act dress. I had one washing machine already going with some fabrics for Fanny's afternoon dresses. I mixed up the dye solution, put the goods for Julie's dress into the other machine, then left to make a phone call. During the interim, someone, not knowing the machine was prepared for use, dropped a purple cloth into it and turned on the switch. I need say no more—except that out came a color I never dreamed I could get had I wanted it; I didn't know it existed.

After the fabrics had been dyed, their colors and shades juggled to my satisfaction, they were taken back to the wardrobe and given to the cutter. It had been explained to her how the garments were to be cut and how they were to be finished off. I became very "nitty-picky" about these details, again, not only because the house is so small, but because a garment—no matter how beautiful the plate— will not work unless it is properly cut and finished. And consistency of stitching must be apparent throughout the costumes. In this production, since the skirts were bias-cut, hemming was exceedingly difficult. Due to the way the fabric was draped on the figure, the hems wanted to go their own uneven way. All of them were rolled hems, so I had them done by hand to avoid that hard-rolled look.

36

Finally we came to the finishing work. A number of dresses required beading and jewels. Since the show would run four weeks before going into "rep," everything would have to stand up under hard wear and innumerable cleanings. Therefore, the beading and the jewels were applied with the utmost precision: each bead, each jewel, was stitched-and-knotted twice.

Then we had to select the accessories. In "The Royal Family," shoes, handbags, hats, and gloves are vital components of the overall motif. I do not like putting trim and jewelry on a costume just for the sake of the trim and the jewelry themselves. They must be relevant to the design of the garment and, in turn, to the entire production. Julie's second act suit is done in luggage brown. Finding a handbag the proper color to enhance the suit was one problem, but added to that was the difficulty of finding one typical of the period. We could not afford to have a period handbag manufactured.

When it came to shoes, we were fortunate in having the cooperation of an excellent local bootery. Since the T-strap is still popular to a certain extent, they were able to achieve the desired effect with just a few changes —a spooled heel, for example, added to an already fashionable last.

It is almost impossible to find a good milliner outside of New York. A designer is lucky if he finds one at all,

Virtually all the costumes for Center Stage productions are made in their own costume shop.

and he has hit the jackpot if he finds one who can follow instructions so the results won't send the cast streaking out of the wardrobe in hysterics. To offset this hazard, our wardrobe staff at Center Stage makes all the headwear for period plays.

After the costumes had been built, shoes selected, hats done, I advised the hairdresser regarding proper coiffeurs. These were then discussed with the cast in consultation with the hairdresser. This area needs constant supervision in any production and can be one of the touchiest jobs.

As for the men's costumes, the consideration that determined them was the same as the women's: achieving the correct silhouette. I spent many days running to outlet houses, good second-hand stores, and the factory outlets here in the city, looking for the right suits, blazers, and trousers. These were then brought back to the theatre and re-styled—in some instances, re-dyed. The men's accessories were also chosen with exacting care—neckties, topcoats, gloves, and so on. It is no less important that the gentlemen of the company be comfortable in their costumes.

I think the most important thing a designer learns from working in a regional theatre is speed and accuracy. In addition, he learns to train his mind to sustain colors, fabrics, and characterizations. While he is actively working on one show, ideas for the next production are forming in the back of his head. And, of course, his overall goal is to maintain a high level of artistry through an entire season.

*Methodology, the by-product of fre-
quently repeating a process, is the
foundation of all craft — if in fact
methodology and craft are not synony-
mous. At Washington, D.C.'s Arena Stage
Company, the costume department,
headed by Marjorie Slaiman, has designed
a vast variety of productions over the past
several years — including several notable
world premieres. What equipment, stock,
and procedures the department maintains
to costume these productions provides a
clear insight into the daily methodology of
a designer for a regional theatre.*

*Marjorie Slaiman began her professional
career as a clothing designer, moved into
acting, and eventually into costuming for
the stage. Before joining the Arena Stage
Company, she designed for several other
theatre groups in Washington. She designed the costumes for "Musical Theatre
Cavalcade," which opened the Wolf Trap
Farm Park for the Performing Arts — the
country's first National Cultural Park —
outside Washington, D.C.*

*The interview, first published in "Theatre
Crafts" magazine in October 1971, was
conducted by Glenn Loney, a contributing
editor and a Professor of Theatre at
Brooklyn College. A member of the
editorial boards of "Theatre Today" and
"Players," he contributes regularly to
"Cue," "After Dark," "Opera News," and
"Dance Magazine."*

Managing a Regional

by Marjorie Slaiman

In recent years, repertory theatres across the country
have come to play an ever-increasing role in the development and premieres of new productions. The unsung
heroes of these productions are the well run, productive
shops of each repertory theatre. The costume shop at
Washington's Arena Stage Company is one of the most
active of all these facilities.

In the 6 years that costume designer Marjorie Slaiman
has been resident designer with the Arena Stage costume
shop, her Washington credits have included the world premieres of "The Great White Hope," "Edith Stein," and
"Pueblo," as well as the world professional premieres of

Theatre Costume Shop

Lucy
Paris, Vel d'hiver.

Lucy - I.2

Negro woman -
Café de Champion

"The Night Thoreau Spent in Jail," and the American premieres of "Indians" and "The Ruling Class." The latter opened the new Kreeger Theatre addition to the Arena Stage complex early in 1971.

The Shop: Equipment, Staff, and Policies

The new addition has meant some changes in the set up of the costume shop. Strolling through the work shop of the Arena-Kreeger complex, Marjorie Slaiman points out the new facilities and their equipment.

"With the new theatre, we now have costume storage in a huge room in the new building, so we've been able to enlarge our shop here. We had the carpenter's shop build us an extra cutting table, mounted on wheels, and we can push it against the old cutting table and have double the space for drapes and large capes.

"Underneath are bins and drawers. We don't throw anything away. The bins contain remnants of material. We buy show-for-show and only carry a stock of very plain materials — like muslins or simple colors — fabrics that can be used at any time. So bits and pieces help. Sometimes ¾ of a yard of something — dyed and fixed — can become a hat or a pair of booties.

"We used to have a problem about work in progress. We didn't have any place to put it aside or away, when other things took precedence. We tried plastic boxes, but they tended to fall apart. So, now each girl has her own cubby hole.

"We have five sewing machines; one or two little portables that are not very useful (because you have to keep setting them up and taking them down) and three industrial or power machines. They are very hardy and do leather and quilting, but with a change of needles they can also stitch silk.

"We've put in two industrial steam irons. We were using plain old home irons, but the mortality rate was great. You pay $16 for an iron, and it lasts maybe 3 or 4 months! And then it is out of commission. You see, we turn them on and leave them on all day so they will be ready whenever we need them. That does tend to burn out an ordinary iron. But these steam irons are just marvelous."

Also included in the inventory of this well equipped shop are, of course, dress forms. But, as designer Slaiman comments, "we don't need to use them very often. We're in close proximity to the theatre, and we can call on actors for fittings. When the time comes, we submit a list of who is needed every morning, and the actors drift in when they are free from rehearsals. It's better that way. We just wouldn't have room for all the forms otherwise."

Other physical facilities of the shop include a table for bindings, tapes, ribbons, sequins, beads, hand work, and a closet for millinery — hatblocks and steamer.

To keep things going, the shop has a staff of four girls. "One is my assistant — she does a little more specialized work," notes Marjorie Slaiman, "but essentially, we're all equal in terms of skill. And when the work has to be turned out, we're all here doing it. Plus Marty Jenkins, a lady who volunteers her time to come in and help during rush periods. Marty is an elderly lady — I guess about 74 — who's been here since the theatre was founded. She refuses to accept any pay — but since she lives quite a distance, we pay her taxi fare to the theatre."

Talking about a few matters of shop policy, designer Slaiman comments, "Our staff is small and our shows are a mixture of built, bought, rented, sometimes even borrowed costumes. We are as economical as we can be. We use our stock as much as possible. We wouldn't go out and buy shirts, for instance, unless we had none of the right size or style on hand. And we can dye them, alter styles, even change the sizes slightly. We often make arrangements with the actors, if the clothes are contemporary, that they pay a portion of the cost of a suit or sports outfit. Then, when the show is over it belongs to them. We have arrangements with some shops and with a tailor. And we usually get clothes for about ⅔ the regular cost so it works out well for us and for the performer.

"In building costumes, of course, patterns are very important. We make them out of brown paper. We do use some commercial patterns, I must admit — for a pair of pants, or something like that; we don't stand on ceremony. If it's a simple pattern, it's foolish to take a girl's time — it could take three hours to draft a pattern. However, for something like pants, if we can get what we want cheaply enough, we will buy them rather than build them."

43

The Finished Product

Of the premieres for which Miss Slaiman has designed and built the costumes, "The Great White Hope" is now something of a theatre legend. No Broadway producer wanted to tackle Howard Sackler's play owing to its huge cast, its many scenes, its myriad of costumes, and its prickly theme. But, Zelda Fichandler, artistic director of the Arena Stage Company, saw the show's potential and threw the theatre's resources — and some grant money — into the project. Under the direction of Ed Sherin, the

The repertoire of costumes developed by Marjorie Slaiman's costume shop at the Arena Stage includes built, bought, rented, and donated clothing. A period ball gown (above) and ecclesiastical attire (right) graced "The Ruling Class."

Washington staging was so much admired that it was brought to Broadway with much of its original cast. The New York production repeated the Washington success and went on to a film sale.

But in New York, there was no credit or designer's fee for Marjorie Slaiman, the inventive and energetic lady who had provided some 247 period costumes for about 160 characters. As Miss Slaiman tells the tale, she was to have done the Broadway show, but her ethics got in the way. As a result she had to wait until the New York premiere of Arthur L. Kopit's "Indians" to get that Broadway credit which a designer seems to need in order to be nationally known.

"Indians"

"Indians" did not, unfortunately, have a very long run on Broadway, but it still enjoyed a great deal of publicity and a number of thoughtful reviews, and the Slaiman costumes for "Indians" were often singled out by reviewers for their dash, style, and appropriateness. On an effectively empty stage, with only some flashing lights and constructivist details for a setting, the actors had to hold the stage by force of character and costume.

If "Indians" soon departed, memories of Miss Slaiman's art did not. Her costumes were named best of the year in the theatre annual, "Best Plays of 1969-70." Also in 1970, Marjorie Slaiman's name was third in the yearly "Variety" poll of drama critics for Best Costume Designer.

Oddly, "Indians" was originally staged in London, but as Miss Slaiman indicates, the designs for that production showed "that English designers knew nothing at all about cowboys and Indians."

"To understand what the Arena Stage's "Indians" was like, you have to know something about the director, Gene Frankel. Gene is a very creative guy — and he's easy to work with because he is visually oriented. He can translate what he wants into a few words, or gestures. I got the script, studied it, and then went to talk with him. I've now worked with Gene twice ("Indians" and "Pueblo"), and both times he has wanted something a little removed from reality.

45

"Gene wanted some very spooky effects—based on reality, but larger. I did all the necessary research for "Indians." I had a whole stack of books on Indian tribes of North America which included a very good magazine plate showing Indians in masks and Gene indicated that was something like he wanted. So I translated what the plate had to say about masks, and we made them here in our shop. It was, in fact, a complicated process. I assigned one girl to make some of them by the slow process of building them out of celastic. Then I painted, furred, and feathered them. Others we've made from balsa wood.

"Frankel also wanted a certain atmosphere of nakedness in the Indian chorus. There our problem was to get white actors to look like Indians. In order to do that we had to get enormous amounts of Texas dirt from the Dallas Texas Dirt Company—the real stuff is not something you buy in any old costume shop. Every night we had to paint these "Indians" completely from head to foot in reddish-brown dirt.

"I provided the chorus only with leather loin cloths. And

Indian headdress (right), fringe (top), beads, and tribal masks (facing page) were freshly researched for Arthur Kopit's play "Indians". All were made in the Arena Stage costume shop, as was Buffalo Bill's fringed jacket (above, middle).

since their movement was choreographed it was all very effective. I gave them blankets for certain dance sequences. I dyed ordinary surplus Army blankets different colors—red, green, grey. Then sewed felt symbols onto each blanket and scraped them down. They had to have a mysterious quality. The effect—with the sounds, lights, and costumes—was impressive.

"For the soldiers and cowboys, we rented costumes. We didn't want to fill the stage with musical comedy cowboys in bright, new duds. They had to be real, and their clothes had to look faded. I rented some things from Western Costumes in Hollywood. But I asked for jackets that were worn and torn. I sent them my sketches and some descriptions and they found very good things for me.

"There were certain prototypes in the show: Jesse James, Wild Bill Hickock, and Buffalo Bill. I put Jesse James entirely in black. For Stacy Keach, who played Buffalo Bill, I made two jackets that required careful work. One was a rough, woodsy, reddish-brown suede jacket. We got the skins, painted them, cut them, made fringes, and turned the jacket out in this shop. Stetson had donated lots of hats, one of which Stacy took as his "rough" kind of hat. Then they sent us a beautiful white hat which he wore in his big scene. That scene was what I made the second leather jacket for. Using acrylics and leather paint it was painted with a design abstracted from the decoration on one of Buffalo Bill's own jackets.

"For the Broadway production I "upped" this jacket by painting it again, and colorfully beading the design. A lot of the costumes in the two productions were the same because many of the actors were in both. I did add one thing to Stacy's costume: a very big, rough coat, made of leather and lined with fake fur—it was supposed to be buffalo.

"The celastic masks that we had made here at the Arena wouldn't work on Broadway because the choreography was altered and the Indian chorus was smaller."

Stars and Bars on the Pueblo

Despite the fact that "Pueblo" (the story of Commander Lloyd Bucher's ordeal with the North Koreans and with the U.S. Navy) looks like a simple show, Miss Slaiman indi-

48

cates that it was tricky.

"I don't think most people who have seen it understand just how difficult it was. For example, ordinarily accuracy in detail might not matter for the Naval Board of Enquiry. But ours is an arena stage and people are quite close to the actors; they can see every detail. Also, this is Washington where people are very rank conscious. Getting the medals and decorations correct for everyone involved turned out to be a much larger, more difficult project than we anticipated.

"We have a whole closet of Navy uniforms that have been donated to us, but they wouldn't do as they were. Some were too small for the cast. Some additional ones had to be rented. Using a book of Navy uniform regulations, we had to replace the gold braid – which we found cost a lot of money. (Downtown at an Army-Navy supply store Rear Admiral's gold braid costs $30.) We had to have hats too. So using the real thing was no money saver.

"As for the North Korean captors, I sent some of the girls to the Library of Congress to do research. We found some very good descriptions of cuts, colors, and fabrics and photostatted copies of Chinese uniforms on which the North Koreans' uniforms are based.

"One thing I ought to point out about the costumes for the North Korean prison guards is the way the hats are cut – very close to the face. That minimizes the make-up problems for white men trying to look Asian. In effect, the problem was more complex still because they were doubling as North Koreans and as Navy men – making changes in a matter of seconds."

49

The Arena Stage

Talking about the differences in working in repertory theatre at the Arena and then taking a production to New York (as they did with "Indians") Miss Slaiman points out, "I enjoyed doing "Indians" more here than in New York. It's the nature of theatre in New York. The pressures you work under, the other people you have to contend with. Most New York theatres have absolutely no facilities at all. There was no work room, no place to go. I had to use Nancy Potts' work room at the Lyceum to turn out the

For the Arena Stage's production of "Pueblo," (below) donated uniforms were refurbished with new gold braid, and hats for North Korean prison guards were cut close to the face to minimize oriental eye makeup (above and facing page, top left).

50

Zany period costuming was required for "You Can't Take It With You" (right). Ecclesiastical and military costumes of World War II vintage were required for "Edith Stein" (below).

Turn of the Century street wear and military uniforms were
the order of the day for Strindberg's "Dance of Death"

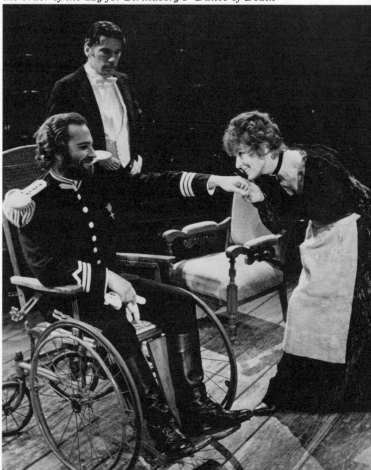

extra things we needed—Stacy's buffalo coat and an extra jacket.

"When the Western rental outfits for the cowboys and soldiers came in, I had to use the shop as a landing place. Spraying or basting or seam ripping had to be done behind the Men's Room door. In New York, you feel that many people—directors, for instance—are working in theatre only for the money in it, or for the credit of a New York production. But their hearts aren't in it.

"In New York you have to fight for every little thing, for every extra. Here, I just take it for granted that we'll make everything the best we can. For instance, I had to give *orders* in New York that I wanted a costume to look a certain way or an actor to wear a certain thing. I'm not interested in an actor's reaction to it. We know that it works successfully. I must say, however, working in New York was an interesting experience.

"Here at the Arena, we give everything we have to each production. We're not doing it for the money. It is an artistic endeavor. That starts with Zelda Fichandler, who guided our production of "Indians" every inch of the way. Every production is a real thing, a perfect entity that we try to achieve. That's why we work for intensive periods and then relax. We work like demons getting a show ready. But, now that we've opened "Pueblo," the major construction and preparation is done. We've earned a bit of a rest— and you don't see many technical people around."

In case anyone is wondering how and where to get the kind of training that equips a costume designer and builder to deal with the problems that come up in repertory theatre workshops, one answer is obvious—by working as an apprentice in a regional theatre like the Arena Stage Company.

53

Costume rental houses are the repertory theatres of the costume field. They are the ever-ready savings banks of continuing costumes—and unfortunate overdrafts seldom occur. Durability and continuity, therefore, are virtually as important as style to them. In fact, durability in both fabrics and styling cannot be overlooked by any costume designer. Also, our costume rental houses are testing grounds for costumes and—what is not so often discussed—a training ground for designers as well. For them, the scope of design opportunities is even more vast than for designers in repertory companies.

Leo Van Witsen tells of his work as resident designer of the Brooks-Van Horn Costume Company, where he heads the Opera Department and serves as a member of the Board of Directors. A native of The Netherlands, he was trained in Paris and Berlin as a fashion designer. He maintained a design studio in The Hague until 1938 when he came to the United States. In this country he has designed an impressive number of pioneer opera projects and has been the staff costume designer for the Goldovsky Opera Theatre since its inception in 1946. He has served as a faculty member of both the Juilliard School of Music and the Berkshire Music Center.

The following article was first published in "Theatre Crafts" in September, 1969.

54

Feathers for Bird Costumes Are for the Birds

by Leo Van Witsen

The opportunities of a resident designer with a theatrical costume firm whose stock includes over two hundred thousand costumes, provide the chance to be creative with new designs as well as to use ingenuity in restyling and maintaining rentable costumes. It can be one of the most versatile jobs in the world of costume.

A resident designer's assignments in a theatrical costume firm are varied and many. Such firms are approached to design just about everything that people (or sometimes animals) wear — not only costumes for drama and opera, but also those for school mascots, Mardi Gras celebrations, waitresses, dolls, and wax figures.

Since rentals comprise the bulk of a costume company's business, the major obligation of a designer is to create "new for rental" costumes. Our costume stock is our capital. It is important for a designer to produce sturdy garments — made with strong fabrics, non-ravelling seams, and hardy linings — that will withstand the rigors and ravages of incessant dry-cleaning, alterations, handling, and wear by non-professionals. It is not so difficult to design a long-lasting costume when brocades, woolens or sturdy cottons are used, but it can be a challenge to create something durable out of chiffon or organza.

Unlike a free-lance designer who can insist that his costumes be hand embroidered, or his skirts cartridge pleated or his fabrics match-dyed for his desired effect, a designer for a costume firm — or a repertory or community theatre group — has a different set of guide rules: to create maximum designs for minimum cost! Although I sometimes envy the free lancer's opportunity to use lavish fabrics and trimmings, I have become rather accustomed to shoestring budgets and there is much satisfaction in accomplishing sumptuous effects with small means. However, resident designers must constantly use good judgment in order to prevent the loss of quality and beauty, for economizing can be overdone. For example, if the use of fur is requested, the designer's experience justifies the use of real fur instead of synthetic copies, which will become quickly matted and ugly. Certainly each design should have an individuality so that everything doesn't look the same.

Not only do we at Brooks-Van Horn design new costumes for new shows and new events but we sometimes design five or six sets of costumes for a Broadway show that has become popular with schools, colleges, and amateur groups. It is a triumph to make sets of "My Fair Lady" ball gowns of the 1912 period, with their long trains, draped hobble skirts of sheer fabrics and laces in such a way that they will not be returned from the cleaners resembling a bunch of tangled rags.

Opera Costumes

Perhaps more than any other assignment, the design of opera costumes taxes the ingenuity of a resident designer. The problem is: *Money.* Opera is expensive, yet small opera companies above all costume renters have the least money to spend, although they need the most sumptuous outfits. But ingenuity can go just so far before the frayed edges begin to show, and this is where other design work helps us out. For example, assignments such as cre-

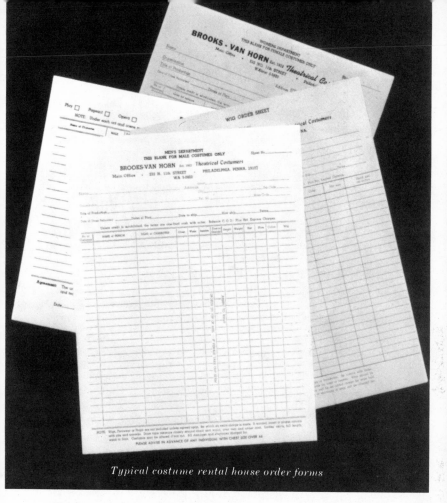

Typical costume rental house order forms

ating costumes for Mardi Gras groups have become practical additions to our opera rental supply. Mardi Gras clubs have now been persuaded to use costumes of less gaudy colors and garish trimmings than was their custom, so that upon return we can use them for opera purposes. One club accepted our suggestion for the theme of "The Triumph of Maximilian I," and subsequently these same gorgeous gowns were used for performances of "Meistersinger," "Faust," "Mephistopheles," "Rigoletto," and "Anna Bolena." It is even more exhilarating, however, when a resident designer can create new costumes for new opera productions. I have recently designed new costumes for "Carmen" and "Fledermaus," which have become valuable assets to our rental stock.

Although a resident designer may consider one form of design his forte, as I think of opera, he must be versatile enough to handle anything that comes along (and almost anything does). But I meet my Waterloo in recreating authentic military attire. Fortunately, in our organization there are others who have a wide knowledge of uniforms and whose eyes light up at the mention of the word "uniform."

I started my career as a fashion designer and to this day some of my many opera-singing friends ask me to design concert-gowns for them. One recent assignment in this genre was to create a gown for mezzo-soprano Betty Allen who was soloist in Mahler's Symphony No. 3 which Leonard Bernstein chose for his farewell performance as conductor of the New York Philharmonic. I consider this a great honor.

Mascot, Utility, and Wax Museum Costumes

Colorful, gay, school mascot costumes, whether they be a falcon, a Viking, a bison, a crocodile, or a "robin with a sneer" must be attractive as well as sturdy. When these mascot apparels are returned for repair, they frequently look as if they have been in battle — one crocodile returned for resuscitation was minus its left rear foot, its claws, and most of the fangs, and its tail was badly mauled! Obviously, for bird costumes, real feathers are for the birds!

Another challenge for resident designers is "utility" costumes. Recently, a big hotel in Philadelphia that dresses its personnel in pseudo 18th Century attire decided to move with the times and deck out their cocktail waitresses in saucy uniforms. It proved gratifying to turn on the "instant design switch" and make 18th Century, Kelly-green frocks in today's mini-skirt lengths which were simple, unfussy, practical, easy to clean, and at the same time flattering to all types of figures (waitresses are not hired through model agencies). The hotel management and the waitresses were delighted with the results.

The project of costuming porcelain dolls could age a designer ten years because of the fear of breaking the dolls, but it has proved exciting to design costumes for two beautiful Martha and George Washington figurines, only two and one-half feet tall.

Wax museum costumes have also been stimulating and challenging. Although I am not an avid admirer of Madame Tussaud's, most wax museum customers are wonderful people. These wax figures have included Tahitian royalty, Inca priests, Knights of the Garter in full regalia, and silent-movie stars. Such commissions can send the designer to the library for enjoyable research.

It is important that the resident designer have a good rapport with his work rooms and the fellow craftsmen in his organization. Fortunately my firm is blessed with a group of magnificent workers (a hard thing to come by in this day and age) who take pride in their craft and who feel secure in their fields of endeavor. More concerned with the end results, no one insists that his is the only way.

While a free-lance designer is on the payroll of the producer — whether for a legitimate play, a TV series, a circus, or a night club — he must also please the director and the stars. Naturally, he hopes that the success of one venture will lead him to future assignments. Sadly, the failure as well as the success of a show rubs off on a designer's reputation. If the costumes are magnificent, but the show a flop, the latter is all that people remember. The impressiveness of the costumes is lost as a credit.

The opportunities of a resident designer with a theatrical costume firm, on the contrary, always provides the chance to be creative with new designs as well as to use ingenuity in restyling and maintaining rentable costumes. He does not have to worry about the success or failure of a show. And although designing for theatrical productions and opera may be the main portion of his creativity, he is constantly presented with a plethora of other interesting assignments. Each of these designs presents a challenge.

59

Circus parades, animal acts, traditional clowns and trapeze artists are costumed in so stylized a manner that they may seem stirred out of an instant-costume package. Not so. Max Weldy reveals the mysteries of the magical world of the circus costume designer and his surprisingly broad activity. Thematic continuity, color co-ordination of different but simultaneous acts and durability—for at least one season—are some of designer Weldy's tightrope design problems. He reveals a sprightly world that is also unknown to most costume designers.

Born in Paris, Weldy designed his first costumes for the Follies Bergere. He designed for such lavish productions as "George White's Scandals," "Earl Carroll's Vanities," and for countless films. Until his recent retirement he was the designer for the Ringling Brothers, Barnum and Bailey Circus, which is the basis of the following interview, first published in "Theatre Crafts" in May/June, 1967.

60

Costumes for the Circus
an interview with Max Weldy

THEATRE CRAFTS: How did someone who designed costumes for the Folies Bergere become associated with the circus?

MAX WELDY: That's right, the first show I designed was the Folies Bergere, and as a matter of fact, I stayed with them until the war. In 1939, John Ringling was in London. I was working there at the time and having an especially good year. Everywhere he went in London, he saw my name. He contacted me in my London office, followed me to Paris, where I also had an office, and finally, when we came close to terms, he told me, "I won't make any definite deal with you until you have seen my circus." So from Paris I had to go to St. Paul, Minnesota; from St. Paul to London, where I was working on a show for the Palladium and from London back to Paris to create and build the costumes. I sent all the costumes for the circus from Europe without having any specific sizes.

T.C.: You must have had some guide lines?

MW: Surprisingly, circus people are all about standard in size. I mean, the acrobats all have a certain build, the showgirls all have approximately the same measurements, and so on. Of course, all the costumes were fitted anyway.

TC: Have you found any differences between designing for the theatre and designing for the circus?

MW: In the circus we have no backstage, there is only this big space, and if anything really separates the circus from the theatre, it's this. Also, we can't rely on a play to captivate an audience. The people come to see a circus which means, more or less a parade. A parade of continuous action that has many centers of activities.

TC: Is there a theme to the circus? That is, do you think in terms of a complete concept?

MW: Yes, for the whole show, I have a complete concept in mind. The theme is most apparent in the grand parade and the rope number. For these, I have to try to find something different each year. But the theme doesn't affect the single acts. Of course, all the performers are in the parade and they have to wear the costumes I design for them according to the theme. Sometimes, I have to use a lot of persuasion.

TC: When do you start planning for the show?

MW: I have to start thinking now about next year. Actually, I'm working all the time. If I get an idea when I'm traveling, I put it on a slip of paper and keep it for future use.

TC: How about the clowns' outfits?

62

MW: The clowns generally have their own costumes. It is a tradition for them. They get famous with a certain look and they have to keep it.

TC: You mentioned that the individual act costumes are not part of the theme. Do you still have a hand in their design?

MW: I design all the costumes. If we have, let's say, three acts of the same kind, I figure out color coordinates for all three. All the people who are in the ring at the same time have to be thought of as an ensemble in so far as the color of their costumes is concerned. With so much happening at once, we cannot create too much visual confusion with clashing colors.

TC: How about the costumes for the animals—are they your responsibility?

MW: Yes. Absolutely. For instance, the camel this year is a dragon, and the llama is a turtle. There are no limits to what you can do. There are some considerations for the animals. For example, you cannot cover their heads.

TC: The circus has always seemed to be steeped in tradition and filled with superstitions. Do either affect your costuming?

MW: Yes, they both do. For example, most high wire artists are Spanish and these performers always appear in a toreador's costume. Trying to change this, to bring in something new, will lead to endless discussions. They will tell you, "My father wore this and he told me, don't change." Or, "you look good in this." Most artists are very superstitious. There are even some colors I cannot use on them. If they had bad luck while wearing a certain color, that color is out forever. The color that is most objected to because of these superstitions is green. Many artists stay away from purple, too.

TC: Do you have to be careful of what effect certain colors may have on the animals?

MW: No, not generally. Of course, the animal trainer stays away from too flashy colors.

TC: What do you find to be your biggest problems?

*Circuses often have an overall theme for the costuming that is
most clearly seen in the grand parade (above).*

MW: There is only one problem: the costumes have to be
workable. They have to withstand some fierce punishment.
Sometimes I am unable to see an act before I design the
costumes. This happens when the artists come from countries where it's difficult to get a passport.

TC: How do you compensate for the "fierce punishment"
the costumes have to withstand?

MW: I am constantly on the look-out for new materials.
We use only the best materials, but we have to buy in big
quantities. And if we want one costume in one specific
color which isn't used for any other costume, it gets very
expensive. I buy all the material for the costumes in the
States, but for a long time I had to import a stretch material I wanted from England. That's about it. I start with
the best materials.

TC: How long do the costumes last?

MW: One season, unless there are accidents and except
for one or two numbers which are so tough that they use

up more than one costume during a season. For example, even if we make the costumes for the bicycle act with double seats, they wear through and have to be replaced.

TC: Have there been any major changes in the costuming over the years?

MW: Well, people are not built the same way any more. They are taller and slimmer. It is funny—if artists come from East European countries, they start out pretty sturdy, but after one year I cannot use the same measurements for their costumes any more—they become slim. A big part of the audience is teenagers; so the show has to be modern. This also carries back to the performers. For instance, years ago the leotards that performers wore were quite long. You had to fight for every inch you wanted to take off. Now, everything is very brief, and I'm sure in a little while everybody will be completely covered up again.

TC: Do you stay with the circus during the whole tour?

MW: No, I go out only to see if everything is all right and to find out how the audiences are reacting. This year, the show is simpler, but funnier, and the public's reaction is much better. The children of today are different. They are not interested in Sleeping Beauty or Mother Goose any more. They want to see space men, monsters, and Batman. So we have Batman in this year's parade which, by the way, is called "Alice in Topsy Turvy Land," and we have Alice in a mini-skirt.

A showgirl in sequins and glitter invites children of all ages to Candyland

Buppa the Clown wears traditional extravagant garb (right). Animal costumes are related to the acts in which they appear (below).

Improvisation is the lifeblood of the theatre. Not only is it the fundamental impulse of let's pretend, it is the standard procedure of most theatre operations. Make-do goes hand in hand with make-believe. Across the boards—and behind and under them—the art of making-do sparks the genius of theatre craftsmen. Such limitations as budgetary restrictions force the imagination of designers into ever higher and more inventive realms. As Oliver Goldsmith wrote about the effect of rhyme on poets (before the days of Freud), "For fancy, like a fountain, plays highest by diminishing the aperture." As much as any other area of theatre, Children's Theatre is forced by budget limitations to use imagination and invention, and some of its heights are superb, as the following article from "Theatre Crafts" special issue on Children's Theatre, in March/April, 1971, indicates.

Patricia MacKay, a Smith College graduate, is associate editor of "Theatre Crafts" magazine, vice chairman of the committee on theatre architecture, and a member of the board of directors of the U.S. Institute for Theatre Technology.

Costuming for children's theatre is rarely as elaborate as in Maxmillion Productions' "The Blue Planet" (above), or in the Children's Theatre International production of "Petey and the Pogo Stick," designed by Robert de Mora (below), or in Pick a Pack Players' "Firebird" (right), designed by Ken Johnson.

Dressing Up
for Children's Plays

by Patricia J. MacKay

Children's theatre, for the most part, has been looked on in this country as a stepchild. In the minds of many theatre people, it conjures up visions of weekend and holiday shows, a house of noisy, restless kids, and an endless diet of sugarplum fairy tales and nursery rhymes staged by non-professionals who serve more as a babysitting service than any really theatrical experience. Children's theatre has been treated as a stepchild to be tolerated— but just barely.

71

In reality, there is much more to children's theatre— simply, without *good* children's theatre there is less hope for audiences interested in live theatre in the future.

Current children's theatre takes several forms. It can be theatre for adults with a broad enough appeal so that children are interested, like the annual Christmas run of "The Nutcracker," almost any other ballet, certain "adult" plays, or the circus that comes to town. Television shows and films are often especially for children, as are puppet and marionette shows.

Technically, the term "children's theatre" is based on traditional theatre concepts—a play is presented for an audience of children—some companies include children among their actors, but most professional groups use only adult actors.

However, in few places across the country does a specific children's theatre group have a permanent home. And even a group with a permanent home will tour schools and communities.

In order to make money, touring is a way of life. So, too, is the fact that children's theatre for the most part cannot be considered commercially successful. There is money to be made, but not a great deal. Touring on a budget, then, is the single most important factor influencing all the technical crafts—most particularly settings.

Although the kind, size, and extent of a set is limited by the size of the form of transportation that the performing group can afford, children's theatre costumes are generally light, easily folded, packed, toured, and stored; therefore, like make-up, costume designs for children's theatre are not affected by whether a company tours or has a permanent home. Because of this, many children's theatre companies depend more heavily on costuming than other technical aspects to carry the visual image of their story.

There are few costume designers who work exclusively in children's theatre—there is just not enough money to support them. Maximillion Productions, PART, and most professional touring companies—which are in effect small repertory companies—have worked with several designers over the years, and usually have found one with whom they can work well. This designer becomes more or less the "resident designer" for that group.

Children's theatre groups that have found a home under the protective wing of an established repertory company have several advantages over the touring groups. In costuming, as in sets, often the repertory company's resident designer will design for the children's theatre too. This is frequently the case at Cincinnati's Playhouse in the Park, and the Little Theatre of the Deaf.

More frequently, budgetary conditions in children's theatre force costume improvisation to new heights, as in the Paper Bag Players' use of cardboard boxes, newspapers, lace tablecloths, lampshades, and the like (above).

The very subject matter of the plays in children's theatre gives designers opportunity to do period recreation, animal costuming, ethnic, and flights-of-fantasy work. Examples of costuming for periods of history are Medieval England as in the National Theatre Company's "Connecticut Yankee in King Arthur's Court," 19th Century America in a PART production, "Young Andy Jackson," and fantasy feudalism in the Goodman Theatre's "The Thwarting of Baron Bolligrew." Unfortunately, budgetary considerations have put a rein on what many groups might do if they could. As Prince Street Players' Jim Eiler puts it, "Our costuming is as sophisticated as our budget will allow."

One group that has a generous technical budget (about $5,000 per show) is Children's Theatre International. Their designer Robert de Mora appears to work almost exclusively for Children's Theatre International and his costuming, both in design and execution, is some of the most elaborate in children's theatre. The company's desire that their stories be beautifully wrapped has given de Mora the opportunity to design in a variety of styles and periods such as Japanese Kabuki, turn-of-the-century Holland, the 1860's in New York, Indian and others.

Some of the most complex and intricate work in either children's or adult theatre went into the company's Irish production, written and designed by Robert de Mora— "Big, Little and In Between." Every jacket, sweater, and skirt has two sides, so that the four tinkers telling their stories of giants, leprechauns, and normal-sized folks can change for their next role easily, quickly, and in front of the audience.

In the face of a small budget for costuming, many groups have become very inventive about adapting and using found objects, or transforming and incorporating street clothing into their design concepts.

Irene Corey of the Everyman Players points out in "Children's Theatre Review" that "a small budget is no excuse for poor costuming. Poverty in imagination is the cause for ineffective design and execution." Mrs. Corey stresses that "creative shopping in hardware stores and dime stores is a must." Her own design executions are clearly examples of her philosophy—she has used simple cotton organdy to make lion manes, porcupine quills, and other animal props and costumes.

One of the most inventive and creative groups in children's theatre is the Paper Bag Players. As their name

74

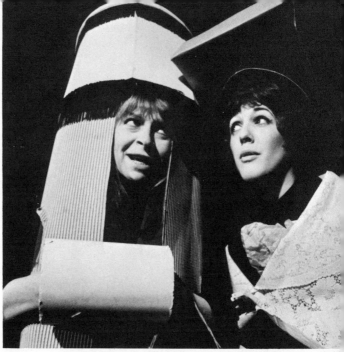

A simple, but evocative costume for a two actor horse immediately conveys the idea of "Circus '70" (below) at Cincinnati's Playhouse in the Park. Found objects, such as corrugated cardboard, a lamp shade, a paint can, a lace table cloth, and an old tomtom as used by the Paper Bag Players are examples of using imagination instead of a large costume budget.

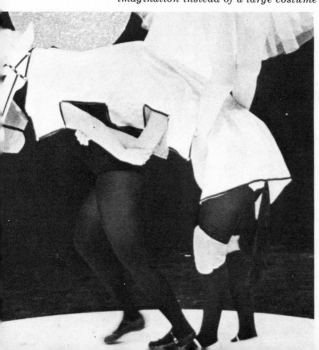

suggests, their approach to costumes is unique, exciting, but carried out with an eye to the budget. Simple brown paper bags and cardboard boxes are the main elements in their costuming. For each dance or skit they start with a general idea of how it should look. Perhaps it should be a brown paper, dancing fish that grows and grows as the actors inside stand up and spread out. Or maybe it should be a lot of boxes to form a crocodile costume. During rehearsal, as the Paper Bag Players walk through and work with the number, they pick up the materials they have around, and start to costume. Often brightly colored acrylic paints add finishing touches to their costume ideas. Found objects, such as corrugated cardboard, lamp shades, a paint can, lace table cloths, and an old tomtom are other examples of using imagination instead of relying on a large costume budget.

Unfortunately, examples of creative uses of materials are far too few. Many groups across the country approach their material with a structured "realistic" vision of what the costume should look like, and end up making do — instead of letting a fresh look at the story and materials at hand work as positive factors in their designs.

Everyone involved in the field has hope that the future of children's theatre will be brighter than its past. The professional touring companies look forward to breaking down the vicious circle of having to tour to make money, but not having enough money to tour with adequate equipment.

In the final analysis, the need for good children's theatre is everywhere evident. Some companies are doing very good things. The majority of companies are not. Theatre for children should be an expanding, enlightening experience, not only for children but for adults to rediscover something lost. It should be creative in its techniques and subject matter — fairy tales in a school gym are hardly relevant. It should be original, in hopes that children can be given some tools with which they will better be able to understand, cope — not just survive — but live with imagination and joy. Hopefully, with the visions of some professionals now working in the field, theatre for children will live happily and relevantly ever after.

Outdoor performances in city environments (above) attract simplified costumes for audiences as well as for performers. For "Midsummer's Morning Madness"—at Cincinnati's Playhouse in the Park—costumes were ingenuously stencilled with each character's name (below, left). Children's Theatre International's "Box of Tears," designed by Robert de Mora, had a more traditional elaborateness (below).

On the fiftieth anniversary of the Bauhaus in 1969, an exhibition that toured the United States and Canada displayed the actual costumes that Oskar Schlemmer designed for that German design schools' dance productions in 1923. To those not old enough to remember them, those costumes were stunning revelations of how far ahead of even our own time its visionary designers were. "Theatre Crafts" began to investigate that influence in the realm of costume design with the publication of the following article in May/June, 1970.

Patricia MacKay is associate editor of "Theatre Crafts."

Man in Space:
From Bauhaus to Moonwalk

by Patricia J. MacKay

During the past year, an exhibition celebrating the 50 years of influence that the German design school—The Bauhaus—has exercised over our environment has been circulating throughout the country. That "50 Years Bauhaus" display coincided, in a strange timely way, with the deaths of the first two directors of the Bauhaus—architect Walter Gropius, and architect Ludwig Mies van der Rohe.

The international influence that the Bauhaus had on architecture, on industrial and graphic design, and on product design of furnishings and fabrics seems not to have been equalled in theatre design. This exhibition brings that fact forcefully into focus.

Seen in this country for the first time, and seldom published clearly, Oskar Schlemmer's costume designs add an exciting dimension to costuming as a whole. For Schlemmer's designs were the genesis of a Bauhaus production; they were the central elements. His costumes determine the movement of a figure on stage. Not until his costuming was complete was the music considered. The size, shape, and even the weight of each costume affected the movement of the figure. What kind of steps a figure could take were important for the composer to know *before* he began. At least one performance of "Triadic" was danced to music for a mechanical organ by Paul Hindemith.

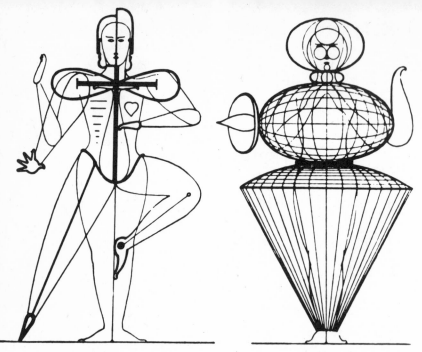

Schlemmer's costume theory diagram of "metaphysical forms of expression" (above left) was "dematerialized" for the finale of the "Triadic" (below left). From his diagram of "the laws of motion of the body in space" (above right) he created the "technical organism" (below right).

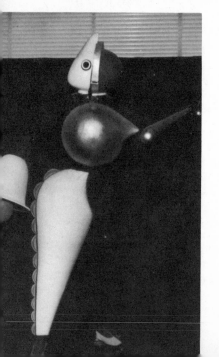

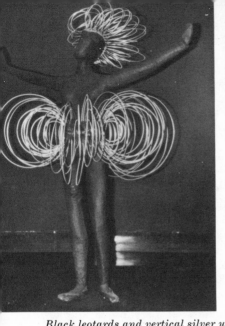

*Black leotards and vertical silver wire hoops formed the costume
for the ballerina (above, left) from the eleventh dance. Suited
up for the yellow series is Schlemmer's realization of
a modern diver (above right).*

The final step was the choreography. As with the music,
the dance could not be finished until the costuming determined how each figure would move in space. Oskar Schlemmer's designs suggest new dimensions—new ways to expand our present concepts of costume, to bring a new
vision to the Seventies.

Oskar Schlemmer made his debut as head of the Bauhaus Theatre School in 1923, during Bauhaus Week, with
a performance of his "Triadic Ballet." (Schlemmer had
originally joined the staff two years earlier as head of the
Sculpture Workshop.) He had been working on his ballet
since 1912, but its first full performance was not given
until 1922. The "Triadic Ballet," with its elements of costuming music and choreography, crystallized the Bauhaus
approach to the theatre.

The "Triadic Ballet" consisted of three major parts:
twelve different dances (divided 5-3-4) were performed in
eighteen different costumes, and danced alternately by
three people—two men and one woman. (Originally
Schlemmer took a role in all of his works.) The first five

81

dances had a burlesque quality and were done with a yellow drop curtain. Included in this series were figures as simply costumed as the almost classically attired ballerina, or as fairy-tale-like as the humpty-dumpty diver of the second dance, or as expressionistic as the over-articulated body of the fifth dance.

The second three dances, in the rose series, were serious and festive. The costuming still related to the body. In the seventh dance the ballerina's tutu was extended in space by hoops that gave her skirt an accordion look; and in the eighth dance, a comical clown and a descendant of an oriental court guard were constructed out of horizontal rings of colored padding.

The final dances had the quality of a monumental and mystical fantasy in black. Here, costumed creatures guided the way on a "mystery tour" of Schlemmer's imagination. They were marvellous creations almost in the realm of total fantasy. Two strange disk creatures danced a duet. There was a trio of two clowns, constructed from huge golden globes, dancing with a ballerina dressed in vertical wire hoops. The figure of the finale was divided, abstract—almost other-worldly.

Schlemmer saw that the art of a "new age" should use the technology and materials of that age. Precision machinery, scientific glass and metal, artificial limbs, the costumes of modern life—from soldiers to sea divers—all play a part in his designs for the "Triadic" and subsequent ballets.

The realism of theatre today has almost entirely discarded masks as a medium of expression. But Schlemmer used them with great success and meaning in his work. Made from papier mache and covered with metallic paint, they were used to intensify expressions, and put the dancers' bodies into a new balance. The mask functioned like a prop that could change and transform the actor's movement.

For the most part all the costumes were constructed out of painted papier mache and padded, stylized tights. Oskar Schlemmer's brother, Carl, was the master craftsman responsible for materializing the original designs.

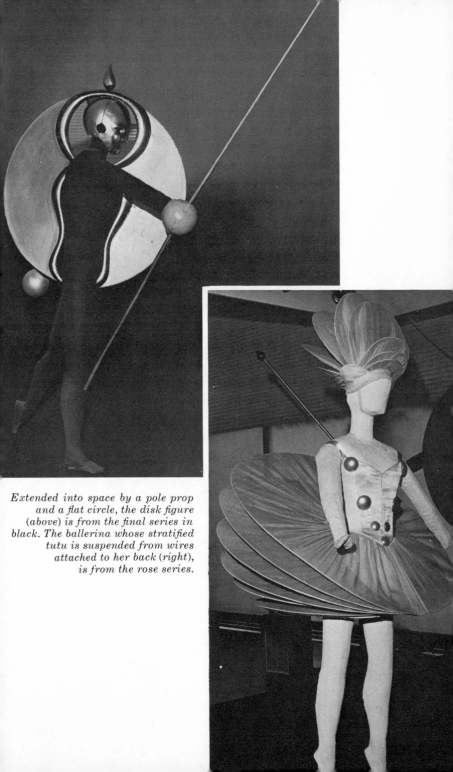

*Extended into space by a pole prop
and a flat circle, the disk figure
(above) is from the final series in
black. The ballerina whose stratified
tutu is suspended from wires
attached to her back (right),
is from the rose series.*

After the "Triadic Ballet," Schlemmer's experiments with costume and dance expanded into other areas. Generally his figures were dressed in stylized tights and masks – a costume that has the effect of unifying the different parts of the body into a simple form. His dancers explored elements in each production: A space dance considered the movement of primary colors on the stage; the form dance explored movement with balls, clubs, and pole props: a gesture dance included murmuring and hissing as well as articulation of the space with pieces of furniture.

Schlemmer's whole approach to costuming – and thus to production – appears to have been forgotten in the rush of pared-and-stripped-down leotarded bodies that followed in the dance world. Alwin Nikolais is the only contemporary designer whose works seem to carry out the potential of Schlemmer's earlier ideas.

At the Bauhaus, theatre developed along the Dadaist lines of parody. Straight plays were somehow suspect, and too pompous. Schlemmer complained that "In our days, which are so very sober and practical, there either is not time left for playing, or else the inclination has disappeared." The only expressions that seemed right were their own dances at the Bauhaus. It was only a quick jete from the foxtrot and jazz to the development of their philosophy about theatrical dancing. It was to be the starting point for regenerating the theatre, because this form of dance was "unencumbered by tradition." Walter Gropius, explaining the Bauhaus Theatre said, "To purify and renew today's stage which, it seems, has lost its intimate ties to the world of human feelings, we are investigating the problems of space, body movements, form, light, color, and sound."

Schlemmer's fascination with space – and with how man moves in it – is the characteristic element of his work. Man is a "space-bewitched creature" whose movements within a certain space are predictable. Not only does each dimensional area have spatial laws, but man's body has inherent spatial laws determined by his physical attributes.

Enter the Costumes. Change the physical attributes of man, by enclosing his body in a costume, and his movement in space will change. Schlemmer saw the principles of costuming as stemming from four approaches to the body—approaches that either stress the body or negate the body almost entirely.

Costumes could be created by transferring cubical forms to the human body—the result would be ambulant architecture. By applying the laws of the body, a costume would exaggerate typical body shapes, creating a marionette. If the laws of the motion of the body in space are used, the resulting costume will be a technical organism. Dematerialization is the result of applying symbolic, metaphysical forms to the body, dividing and suppressing parts of it. The movement of a costumed dancer could be further altered by adding props—extending the body into space with stilts, poles, balls, hats, canes, and so on.

Rooted in this philosophy Oskar Schlemmer's costume designs are striking, and decidedly revolutionary—even today. His work went far to re-evaluate the most basic concepts of costuming. Schlemmer's designs are more than a decorative adjunct to the performer and the performance—they are the force which generates the entire production. Oskar Schlemmer, in the 1920's, was genuinely expanding costuming into another performance medium.

In the 1970's what could new fabrics—plastics, mylar, plexiglass, and fiber optics—or anti-air pollution equipment do to movement in space? What about the zero gravity of a space walk? Maybe Neil Armstrong on the moonsurface with space suit and lunar pack choreographed the most contemporary, relevant ballet!

85

Costuming is only one part of the inextricably integrated theatre miracles of Alwin Nikolais. Known primarily as a choreographer, he also composes his own music and sound—most often on the electronic Moog synthesizer; he designs his own lights, scenery and props, and his own projected scenery, which in his most recent work fuses in an exhilarating ambiguity with the costumes, props, and dancers themselves. His are almost without doubt the finest products of the multi-media idiom.

In costuming he extends the human body and its covering out into space— beyond costume and body—in a Bauhaus manner. His development of this extension begins with the use of props—flexible poles in "Sanctum," buckram shields in "Allegory," metal frames in "Tower," and stretch tapes in "Tensile Involvement." Then, his props virtually take over as costume and the body begins to disappear—as in the box-cages of "Structures," the masks in "Galaxy," and,

87

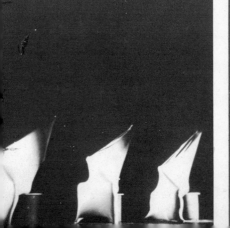

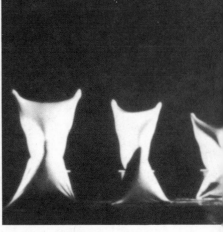

ultimately, the dehumanizing stretch fabric tubes with hoops in "Finials" and the larger, flexible tubes in "Noumenon." In between is the billowing fabric scenery of "Tent," which not only changes fluidly to create varying scenic environments but also menacingly merges with the dancers to become draped costumes. Finally, with projections, in "Echo" and several other works, Nikolais' costumes for both leotarded and stretch-tube figures not only merge with the projected scenery as a single

element but the dancers themselves' are ambiguously dematerialized and fuse with both costumes and sets into a unified revelation that is inexplicably thrilling.

Alwin Nikolais' works have been filmed, televised and have toured all over this country and his Dance Theatre has toured to rave notices throughout Europe. The recipient of two grants from the National Endowment for the Arts, two Guggenheim Fellowships, the Dance Magazine Annual Award of 1968, and the Grand Prize of the City of Paris at the Sixth Annual Paris International Dance Festival of 1968, he has served as the president of the Association of American Dance Companies and as a member of the New York State Council on the Arts. After more than 20 years of association with the Henry Street Playhouse, he recently formed a new school and company association with the Chimera Foundation in New York. The interview was first published in "Theatre Crafts" in November/December, 1970.

an interview with
Alwin Nikolais

Environments
for the
Human Figure

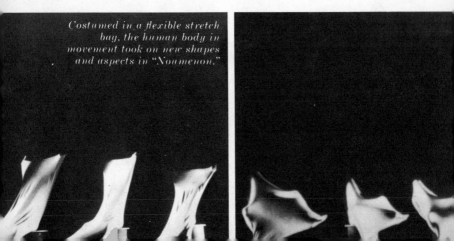

Costumed in a flexible stretch
bag, the human body in
movement took on new shapes
and aspects in "Noumenon."

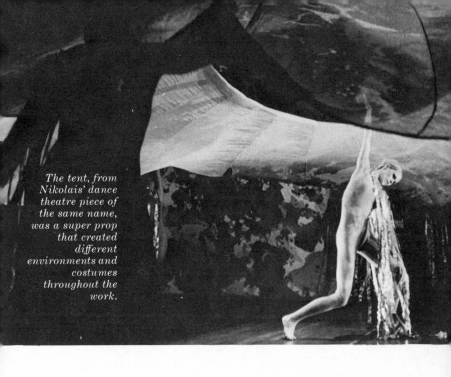

The tent, from Nikolais' dance theatre piece of the same name, was a super prop that created different environments and costumes throughout the work.

THEATRE CRAFTS: We know that when forced to describe your work you often refer to it in terms of a "theatrical environment"—that is everything working together, lights, sound, movement, and costumes. We want to investigate just one aspect of your work, that of costuming.

Marcia Siegel in a "Dance Magazine" article implies that it was in 1948 when you found students unwilling to part with their "treasured self-expression" that you began to give them props and other devices to help them transcend themselves. Was this your first experiment into the use of props in dance?

ALWIN NIKOLAIS: In that particular way, yes. Of course, I had used props before, but more or less like dancers often do. For instance, Martha Graham uses a cup or an ash tray when she has a dramatic idea toward it. She uses props very much as an actress.

TC: How does your approach differ?

AN: In my instance, the prop was not something to be handled as an instrument, but as an extension of the human figure. So that if, for instance, the dancer carried a pole, the pole was like another limb, and it wasn't used like a rake or a hoe.

In the beginning, I gave the problem of props and masks as an extension of the volume of the aura of the dancer as a challenge to my dancers to expand themselves into a greater environmental experience. In the process of doing this, I discovered aspects of theatricality that began to intrigue me, and took me away from the props used as props, or the masks used as masks, into an area of abstraction. All sorts of things and all sorts of points of view developed out of this.

TC: For instance?

AN: One basic thing was a definition to me that dance was not the art of emotion, but of motion. This is very primary to me. Motion precedes emotion. For example, you cannot say that Bach is making his music sigh or cry. He is merely juxtaposing tonalities, one on the other. But, the emotional depth is much stronger than say, MacDowell's "To A Wild Rose."

I am not a modern dancer in the traditional sense of dance being the art of emotion. We are related to modern dance and offsprings of it. My dance isn't emotional in that sense, however, it is in the sense that motion becomes the musicality of the dancer, rather than the actress' narrative emotional process.

In this idea, I discovered in 1948–49 the McLuhan concept of "the medium is the message." That is, the motion itself is the stuff which imparts to the onlooker what you want to say.

There was something else, too. In 1948, dance was also a matter of sexuality. The traditional modern dancer is concerned with Freudianism—in so far as the derivation of all human value was from sexual impulses. I disagreed. I was anti-Freudian. I feel that there are many other impulses and reasons for life. I felt sex was a very lovely thing, but I would like to see what man looked like when he was satisfied.

TC: The use of props in your work goes way beyond simply extending the dancer into space with a prop as Oskar Schlemmer did at the Bauhaus.

'he leotarded body as given props nd extended into pace by flexible oles in Sanctum."

AN: I must say that I didn't know Oskar Schlemmer at the time. A lot of our work has been compared. As a matter of fact, on a European tour recently Frau Schlemmer, who still has the costumes, wanted me to revive one of his ballets. I would have done it except that the plans fell through.

TC: In some cases you and Schlemmer seem to be working in the same areas.

AN: Possibly, yes. But I don't believe that Schlemmer and I are one and the same. We were speaking about environment earlier—I use props differently—they are not just extensions, they are also incidental things in the environment. One of the things that I also came to conclude was that I believe man is not the dominant mechanism of universality. He is a minor but lovely part of it. He must act with grace toward the environment, and in turn the environment may act with grace toward him. There is also interchange. Sometimes he is engulfed by the environment, sometimes he passes through it with dominance. But there was loving interchange. So that my concept here is rather a theatricality of man and environment—but it was all done in metaphor and symbolism so that the lights and designs all work together.

TC: When you start work on a piece where do you begin?

AN: Vision, usually—inner vision. But it is not always very determined. I might have a vague idea in the back of my mind. For example, I'd like to tie a steel disk on a dancer's foot and see what happens. I try to find a Gestalt. Once I have this idea that I want to use something on the dancer then I'll put it on him, work with it until it speaks to me, and then choreograph.

TC: So that sometimes the idea for the costume comes first?

AN: Sometimes. For example the stretchy, flexible bag costume from "Noumenon" I think might have come from the material. What could you do with it? The flexibility and the way that material could be manipulated made the dance come to mind.

TC: You spoke earlier of the areas of abstraction into which props or costumes took you.

AN: Yes, there are certain pieces where I do "de-humanize." One of the first props I used was the bag in "Noumenon." You never see the human figure but just the evolving shapes. I am concerned with the dancer as motivating force for the garment.

94

TC: Does the garment or the dancer determine movement?

AN: Both, because the dancer bends in certain places so I have to make the costumes in certain ways. For instance, the placement of the hoops in "Finials"—there is one around the hip. If it were in a different place the hips might show and defeat the clarity of the final shape; same with the knees.

TC: At what stage of the rehearsal do the dancers begin to work with the costumes and props?

AN: Immediately. The movement is choreographed for the confines of the costume. And, we start with props right

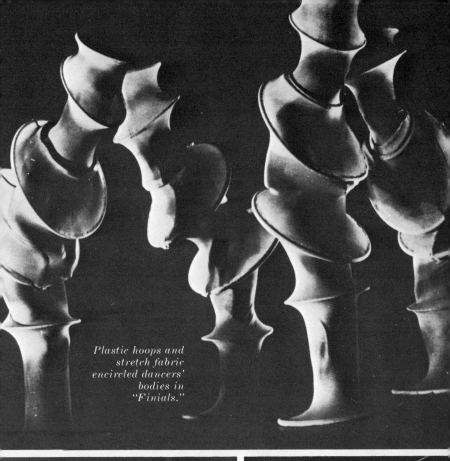

Plastic hoops and stretch fabric encircled dancers' bodies in "Finials."

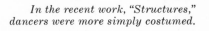

In the recent work, "Structures," dancers were more simply costumed.

Stretch tapes in "Tensile Environment" extend the dancers' bodies into space.

away. The original prop might just have been an indicator of the final. We may change en route because as I'm working with it I may say that a longer pole or a shorter one is better. Everything stays mobile until it happens.

TC: But these abstract costumes are just one aspect of your work, aren't they?

AN: Yes. Customarily the dancer was a dressed figure. In the day when I studied with Graham and Humphrey and Weidman — the men wore pants and shirts and the girls wore dresses. I challenge you to find very many photographs of that period when realism — or rather representational realism — was not the thing. But I wanted the human figure. Curiously, I am accused of de-humanization.

TC: But what about costumes like those for "Finials" or "Noumenon"?

AN: There are only very few like that. Over 22 years of work you would find that about 90% of my costuming is tights, because I like the human body, and the moment you design it, it becomes inflexible. I wanted the human figure. I think perhaps I would have liked it naked, but that didn't entirely suit me so I just used a simple pair of colored tights. But I didn't like the hands and head sticking out. So in one of the first pieces I did, "Kaleidoscope," I designed the face and the hands and the feet in one with the costume so it was a continuation. The leotarded body, with designs structured on the body has been very important in the motional impact of the dance.

TC: Who executes your costumes and props?

AN: I have a tech crew and a tailor who does the costumes.

TC: Do you go out and shop?

AN: I do. Or, I tell my tailor I'd like this kind of thing, or we can go through the samples that he keeps. One of the delights for me is to go down to Canal Street here in New York, and just wander through the plastic and electronic things there. They are very stimulating to me.

TC: What about colors, how do you work with them in your costuming when you have such vibrantly colored slides?

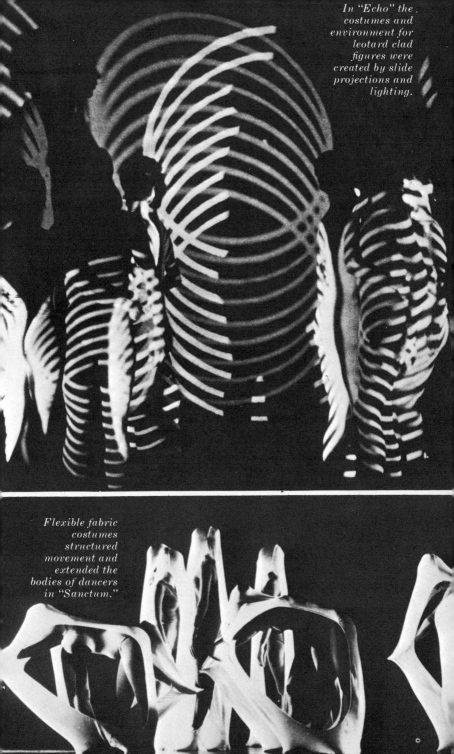

In "Echo" the costumes and environment for leotard clad figures were created by slide projections and lighting.

Flexible fabric costumes structured movement and extended the bodies of dancers in "Sanctum."

AN: That is very difficult to say. It is like asking a musician why he chose to use C# Major. I just have a feeling that I want certain colors and that others won't work. I have been using very pastel colored tights upon which the projections would take—so that the costume colors are only important in so far as they furnish an agreeable screen. The color of light on the body was always, to me, another thing of expressional possibility—that is part of the whole vision. As I have often explained—say, for instance, if I chop my arm through a red light it is not the same as if I chop my arm through a green light. The color is an essential conditioner on the action. In the same way, if I have a sound in my music like "Boom," it is different from a whistle. These are different kinds of musicalities that the theatre offers in that magic box. To see what the aesthetic Rorschach is has always been a great interest of mine.

TC: Have you worked in the round?

AN: Not totally—some in thrust. My costumes are very three-dimensional, but because I am very strong on the visual impact I find that round or thrust tends to limit one. For example, in round you have either the audience or the floor as the background for the performer. They are unchangeable, whereas with a frontal vision, I can hide my lights and put lights anywhere. I can change and make the background a projection. I really think that the thrust and the round stage are more auditory than visual stages.

TC: During a USITT seminar held at the Henry Street Settlement last Spring, you indicated that you felt the whole multi-media thing was dead. What is your feeling about where we are going?

AN: Well, every time I pick up a new college catalogue, multi-media is there, and I don't think that it is here to stay in that sense. I don't believe that multi-media is dead yet, but the minute it starts getting into the academic state, we're going to find that it will have to be made in an academy, and multi-media will go into dead storage. Art changes, and the substance of art changes, and the techniques of art change as the social periods go on. I think in multi-media for some very simple philosophical reasons. One is the idea of the environment which we are becoming very much more sensitive to now. The second is the idea of being unsure of the validity of the message of a single sense. This is the thing that is important. I mean we can't believe what we read, we can't believe what we see or hear alone. You have to be bombarded by all the senses, so that the advance scouts can come back and interplay the message.

I think in a later period we will find another form and this is already evident. I mean the idea of nudity is certainly already a statement away from multi-media. It can be mixed with multi-media, but that is just because of embarrassment, except in "Oh! Calcutta!" where it was plain realism. I think that the idea of realism is not the idea of multi-media. In realism I am not attempting to speckle you with the sun through the leaf environment. I want to see the thing itself, and this is a stage we're in now, too. They're both going on simultaneously.

TC: In your own Dance Theatre are you working more into the realism?

AN: I think "Tent" has a little of it. There is really a symbolism of nakedness. If I had wanted nudity I would have had to choreograph differently for it. The whole thing still agrees somewhat with my idea of the overall involvement of man in environment. That sometimes he disappears in it, sometimes he comes out, sometimes he's naked, sometimes he's covered. So realism and abstraction, identification of the human figure, and loss of the human figure are all wonderful.

99

Turning the tables on the process of costume design is not a typical or recommended activity for designers, but an investigation of one class of materials — usually not the first choices that costume designers make — can open up new possibilities. The effects of plastic materials in the theatre — when used frankly as plastics — are varied, unexpected, and startlingly special. Although some designers and technicians claim that volumes could be written about these current uses of plastics in the theatre, the special issue of "Theatre Crafts" magazine October, 1970, found the information sketchy or buried at the time. The editors do not suggest that costume designers conceive a production by asking how they might use plastics — any more than they would suggest starting with a scheme for the fullest utilization of gimps — but surveys of materials and special methods can uncover a valuable store of information for designers.

For a biographical sketch of Patricia MacKay, associate editor of "Theatre Crafts," see page 69.

Plastics in Costumes

by Patricia J. MacKay

The theatre has always been a scavenger for materials that create desired visual images in sets and costumes. As it stands now, people who are interested in exploring the possibilities of plastics find themselves adapting, piecing together, and playing amateur chem lab. The Metropolitan Opera's David Reppa notes that, "none of the materials we use today were developed specifically for the theatre. We get them by accident or re-application." At the Guthrie Theatre, Property Master James Bakkom and Technical Director Robert Scales have found that most of their foam products come from the building trades —insulation in construction, fill for expansion, weatherproofing, and so on.

Nor is it easy for those groups around the country who have experimented with plastics to let others in the theatre know what they are doing, what they have discovered or discarded.

The people in the field who know about such things— The Society of the Plastic Industry, the various magazines devoted to the exploration of plastic application and

Courtiers from Center Opera Company's "Midsummer Night's Dream" (above) wore costumes hand painted with acrylic based paints. Douglas Campbell as Clytemnestra (below) in the Minnesota Theatre production of "The House of Atreus" wore plastic jewels designed by Tanya Moiseiwitsch.

uses, and the chemical manufacturers themselves—are all hazy about not only where plastics are used in the theatre, but even if they are being used in ways other than the usual domestic applications of rugs, curtains, and upholstery. The chemical manufacturers do not publish or disseminate information for the theatre as they do for construction or automobile manufacturing—and, in general, the middleman supply distributor does not have a big enough budget or voice.

Furthermore, the big chemical manufacturers—those really responsible for developing new plastics for specific applications—don't care about the theatre. In terms of their volume of business, the theatre is just too small to consider. They neither investigate where plastics might be used in the theatre, nor what kind of plastic might be developed to fill certain theatrical needs; nor do they think about the theatre application of the materials that they have already developed. At this time, however, when the American theatre is as diverse and dispersed as it is, it is not an easy market for chemical companies.

The United States Institute for Theatre Technology has been innovative in getting a perspective on plastics within the theatre. They have published vacuum forming information in their journal; and their Midwest Section has held a seminar on stage properties and special effects which dealt with plastics. More recently, the American Theatre Association (formerly AETA) has also held several seminars on uses of plastics in the American theatre and new materials being used in Germany.

The actual role that plastics can and do play within the theatre, however, is still to be explored with more creativity.

In costuming, people have experimented with translucent sheeting and similar materials. Also included in the repertory of sewn, vacuum-formed, and fashioned costuming are flexible and rigid vinyl, Celastic, and foams, such as flexible ethafoam.

Perhaps the most spectacular and familiar use of plastics in costuming is in vacuum-formed, plastic armor. The vacuum forming process is the same for sets but the

103

Robert Israel's designs for "Midsummer Night's Dream" surrounded the stage with inflated vinyl sculptures (above). The costumes for this production of the Minneapolis Center Opera Company production were made of dayglo vinyl. Mylar "space capsule" costumes for the Harpies in the Center Opera production of "To Hellas" were also designed by Robert Israel (below).

Celastic armor protected David Snell, as Henry VI, from the blows of Donald Madden, Richard III, in the New York Shakespeare Festival's "The Wars of the Roses."

rigid styrene or vinyl sheets are molded into helmets, breast plates, masks, spears, and shields. Kate Feller, at Costume Armour, Inc., has found that 80mm Kydex is better than lighter weight vinyl because it will stand more wear. She has also discovered that metallic finishes can be added to the Kydex—cord edges and crests can be applied with a hot glue gun. For touch-ups on Kydex, a plastic base metallic paint like Krylon or Illbronze is best.

In addition to simulating armor, vac-forming is also being used to create jewels and jewelry, crowns and elaborate orders, such as the Order of the Garter or the Golden Fleece. This is where Mattel's 2″ × 3″ toy vacuum-forming machine can be used advantageously.

Celastic

Celastic is another familiar plastic material that has been used to create armor. Very simply, the process of working with celastic involves wetting the material with a solvent which dissolves the stiffener. The damp celastic can then be draped and shaped over a mold or form. When dry, the finished product can easily be painted. The New York Shakespeare Festival armed the Houses of York and Lancaster for a 1970 summer production of "The Wars of the Roses" in this manner.

Frank Messmore of the Messmore and Damon set shop reports that he imports an English equivalent of celastic called Colloid Fab, which has the same characteristics, but is less expensive than the product used by most people.

Plastic Foams

Plastic foams, especially flexible urethane and flexible ethafoam, are being used in various undercover ways in costuming. It makes very convincing padding and is easy to work with. The Metropolitan Opera has sewn pieces of foam onto their costumes to give the effect of heightened relief. Costumer Ray Diffen comments that his shop has used foam to build cog-wheel costumes for a Bulova watch commercial; gear wheels of flexible foam enhanced the effect of watch parts in movement. For the Minneapolis Center Opera Company's "To Hellas," a lightweight and cool styrofoam frame was used to support an Argonaut's unusual costume.

Nylon, Dynel, and Vinyl

Nylon's contribution to costuming is as diverse and familiar as it is to clothing worn off stage. Dynel, a modacrylic fiber, has opened up a whole world of realistic, easy to manage, inexpensive fake-fur coats, trim, and throws.

Vinyl fabrics are also used extensively in costuming. They have the flexibility and working ease of fabric. In addition, vinyl sheds water, resists flame, will stand up well in nightly wear because it is scuff and stain resistant, and a damp cloth will remove dust and grime. It comes in varying thicknesses and can be pressed into numerous patterns, like linen, grass cloth, and straw. It can also be made to look like a shiny, wet-look patent, or left in its matte state. For heavy duty uses, unsupported vinyl sheeting is laminated to a plain fabric backing. The result

A lightweight and cool styrofoam frame supported the Argonaut's costume from the Center Opera Company's "To Hellas" (above). Acrylic mirrors decorated the vinyl cloak of Charles Keating (right) as he appeared in the Minnesota Theatre production of "The Alchemist."

is stronger and has a degree of elasticity. Its main use in costuming is to simulate leather, either as trim or whole costume pieces.

But, as Burton Bell, assistant costumer at Minneapolis Guthrie Theatre points out, vinyl can be and is used in many more interesting ways. In their production of "The Alchemist," supported vinyl and patent vinyl were used to create effects that more conventional fabrics could not have achieved and acrylic mirrors decorated a vinyl cloak in the same production.

Imagination and scavenging are the keys to a number of other special effects that have been accomplished with plastics. Burton Bell tells that when a straw hat that would survive a jump into a vat of water was needed for a production of "Merton of the Movies" at the Guthrie Theatre, their milliner used braided polyethylene garment bags painted with flex glue and French enamel varnish.

Some of costumer Bell's other applications include: for visibility and ventilation in masks, plastic window screening; for jewelry, plastic foam and hot melt glue; for good lace collar stiffener, plastic window shade liquid.

At the Center Opera Company of Minneapolis, inflated vinyl sculptures, dayglo vinyl, and silver vinyl have all been used imaginatively in costuming. Robert Israel's designs for the production of "Midsummer Night's Dream" surround the stage with inflated vinyl sculptures. The costumes for this production were made of dayglo vinyl. Courtiers from "Midsummer Night's Dream" had costumes hand painted with acrylic based paints.

Plastic as Plastic

The plastics used as plastics in costuming include certain vinyls, clear and translucent sheeting, and films of acetate, polyethylene, and mylar. These may be used as just part of a costume or as an entire costume. One drawback of costumes fashioned entirely out of plastics is that the material is hot and does not breathe as cloth does.

Included in the creative application of plastics in costumes are the Center Opera Company's production of "To Hellas," designed by Robert Israel, and the Will Steven Armstrong-designed industrial show for Chevrolet. Israel designed mylar space capsule costumes and Armstrong created whole costumes out of clear plastic with plastic jewels.

What is the future of plastic in costuming? The materials are available—more are being fabricated each year—they only require the right plays, ballets, operas, a creative approach to costume construction, and a designer's vision.

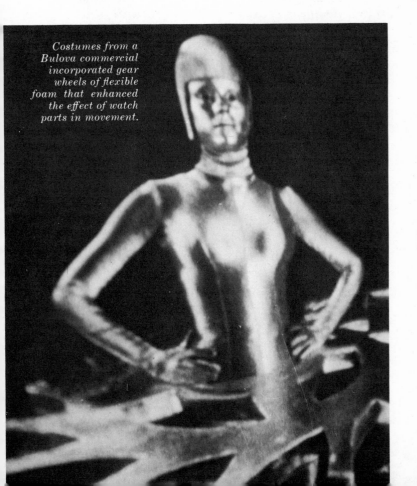

Costumes from a Bulova commercial incorporated gear wheels of flexible foam that enhanced the effect of watch parts in movement.

109

Inexpensive foam rubber and polyurethane sheeting provided a lively experiment in fabrication and an appropriate grotesquerie for an unconventional production of "Peer Gynt." Starting with a common material that is readily available and applying it in uncommon ways can usually produce special results. The following discussion, first published in "Theatre Crafts" January/February 1969, details how it was done.

The author, Barbara Burns Matheson, is a designer, teacher, artist, lecturer, and mother. She studied at Boston University, Harvard, and Radcliffe. She has designed costumes for Tufts University, the Boston Fine Arts Festival, Charles Playhouse, Emerson College, and Rhode Island College, where she currently teaches. She also teaches at the School of Fashion Design in Boston. She has designed for community theatres and for television in the Boston area as well as exhibiting her costume designs and paintings in several one-woman shows. The manager of her own rental and custom costume firm in Auburndale, Massachusetts, she is writing a booklet on "Three Dimensional Costumes."

Polyurethane Trolls
for "Peer Gynt"

by Barbara B. Matheson

Ibsen's "Peer Gynt," is considered a heavy romantic extravaganza, more suited to the idiom of grand opera than to the stage, but last spring, Emerson College presented a low-budget, small stage production of the play with great success.

The tone of the production was highly experimental. We switched the emphasis from romanticism to comedy and, occasionally, to bawdy farce. Instead of following the tenets of nineteenth-century theatrical realism, we made use of all the obvious theatrical conventions. Our criterion was "that which stands for but is not."

This approach to the play meant that, as faculty costume designer, I was free to make crowns out of plastic forks, and turban feathers out of potato whisks. But I still had the problem of numbers: though we had reduced the cast to twenty, each actor had, on the average, seven roles. And there was no escaping the trolls—fourteen of them.

The set designer, who temporarily converted our stage from proscenium to thrust, devised a black and white, al-

The trolls are from Barbara Matheson's production of "Peer Gynt" for Emerson College.

most constructivistic set. After a false start, I adapted the constructivistic principle to the costumes. Everyone wore a basic uniform: white tights, white jerseys, denims, and boots. To this they simply added accessories that suggested their specific roles.

The troll costumes, although they required only heads and body shields, took most of my time. But the job would have been much more difficult had I not known the potential uses of foam rubber.

112

The year before, some slabs of 4-inch thick foam, left over from costume padding, had challenged my creative curiosity. I needed at that time Greek headdresses, beards, crowns, and helmets for "Hippolytus," and I decided to experiment with the foam. Taking a wet sharp knife, I sawed the slabs to size. Then, transferring to scissors, I snipped bas-relief effects into the surface and sprayed it with three colors of paint. The finished products were surprisingly realistic, and the foam, besides being lightweight and faster to work with than celastic, is sufficiently durable. If these objects are stored in plastic bags, away from sunlight, I believe they will last at least four years.

To make the troll heads and shields, I bought sheets of plastic (polyurethane) foam rubber, 38 feet long, 6 feet wide, and 1 inch thick; some 10¢ half-inch brushes, and foam glue. Then I appointed a special troll-building team of seven, headed by Nita Gay, my graduate assistant, and we went to work.

Before we started to build, we tried to get the feel of our materials. We spent hours cutting the foam into strange shapes. We taught ourselves to judge what amount of glue was needed to coat each seam-side, and we perfected our timing so that, without using common pins, we could get the tacky sides to adhere together and could get concave to adhere to convex shapes.

The students watched me make the first head and body shield, and after that, they were quite capable of following the sketches on their own. They even elaborated on them, attaining ever more hideous effects. All were receptive to the possibilities of foam rubber—two of them subsequently designed some beautiful butterfly headdresses, glued onto foam helmets, for another production.

The construction of the heads was simpler than it looks. Instead of carving the features into the foam, we conserved our time by gluing on features taken from latex, joke-shop masks. We obtained different skin textures by adhering materials that reflect light differently—satin and burlap, for example—onto the matte surface of the foam and spraying the result as if it were a collage. For paint we used a quick-drying enamel spray and used the glazing technique of light colors first, dark shadows last, to apply it. So that the trolls could sing, dance, and tumble, we had to provide viewing and voice holes. These were easy to add, however, even after the heads were finished: we simply cut them, then sprayed them a gangrenous color.

We found that Velcro closures, adhered to a seam-butt of least stress, made splendid zippers for the necks of the heads. We originally planned to attach the body fronts to the actors with velcro straps and closures, but during fittings we decided these fastenings would be disconcerting for the audience. Instead, we sewed the fronts with large rug-thread cross-stitches right onto the turtle-neck jersey uniforms. If we had had to provide complete bodies,

113

I think I would have used the same jersey base to avoid the inevitable Velcro zippers up the back.

The body-fronts of the fat, pumpkin-shaped trolls required an extra amount of foam, so to insure that the stitches would hold up under stress, we adhered a cotton lining. Those of the svelter trolls were simply body-cut, princess-styled, with darts adhered. They needed no lining for our purposes, though, for a longer run, they would. A latex coating would also have made the foam more durable, but we couldn't afford it. As it was, we spent only about $119 on the trolls: $50 for foam (we used half our order), $30 for paint, $12 for latex masks, $5 for two gallons of glue, $2 for brushes and $20 for Velcro.

Dress rehearsal was a satisfying experience. The play progresses from "someplace on earth, through dream terrain, to an undefinable presentation of time," and I felt my costumes conveyed this. In the first scenes, the villagers wore contemporary jackets, retrimmed and styled into semi-cut-aways. The maniacs in the madhouse scene were compressed into chrome-yellow jersey tubes, so that their hands stuck out from their shoulders, like walrus flippers. In the funeral scene, where the acting was ritualized, the villagers, with their white faces, white foam millstone collars and pointed tubular hats, looked like chessmen. In the last scenes, all the accessories, which ranged from lampshade hats to shower curtain capes, were plastic; watching the actors perform, I felt I was staring at an absurd, constantly shifting photographic negative.

114

But I was specially proud of the trolls. As the troll princess made her first entrance up through the trap door to begin her seduction of Peer, the audience gasped. Her green cape and cellophane sea-weedy hair covered everything except her enormous chartreuse breasts and abdomen. Her 60–30–60 charms were a triumph of ghastly pulchritude.

"PEER GYNT"

Grotesque masks for
the trolls in "Peer
Gynt" were made of
polyurethane
foam rubber,
cut, glued, and ornamented
with special
"gangrenous" color.

Anachronism has been a theatre tradition since Shakespeare — perhaps even since Aeschylus. Yet costuming a classic play in modern dress can create anachronisms so powerful that they raise questions about the appropriateness of updating. Sometimes an imported period can pervade an entire production — sets, text alterations, music, and costumes; sometimes the updating must be restricted to only one element. William Roberts examines the determining factors in such decisions and explains a minimal refinement in costuming for the history of theatrical anachronism.

William D. Roberts has contributed to the theatre not only as costume designer and scenic designer but also as playwright. Educated at the University of Chicago, Yale Drama School, Chicago Academy of Fine Arts and The Art Students' League of New York, he has been the resident designer of the Charles Street Playhouse in Boston and spent five seasons as resident designer at both the Group 20 Theatre in Wellesley, Massachusetts and the McCarter Theatre in Princeton, New Jersey. His article, first published in March/April 1967, is another revealing analysis of the careful thought process in costume design.

The Contemporaneity
of "Love For Love"

by William D. Roberts

We opened the 1966–67 season of the Charles Playhouse, a season in which we wanted to stress the contemporary aspects of all the plays, with a production of Congreve's "Love for Love." Our first thoughts concerning the physical production were to go all the way—dress it as in "swinging London," 1967. After all, we felt, though on one level the piece is a 17th Century farce and its satire is concerned with matters of that period, on a deeper level, it is a satire on hypocritical attitudes toward sex and money—two subjects which are certainly not dated, and will not be dated, as long as human beings exist.

However, "Love for Love" is a farce; its people not characters but types; its basic situation extremely arbitrary and patterned; its satire achieved essentially through elegantly honed, brilliant dialogue. Its basic style is, therefore, set at once: glittering, decorative, slightly dehumanized, abstract.

117

Sailor Ben (left) and Buckram and Snap (below) had costumes with 17th Century silhouettes but designer William Roberts used a flat, intense contemporary color palette for the fabrics.

One particular hope was, working within this style, to make the satirical points clear to a twentieth century audience. So our first thoughts were to use discotheque music, modern dress, and a lit-up plastic, very abstract set.

As we continued to talk, and reread the play, we discovered our initial ideas becoming obstacles. The play *still* might work that way—it would be interesting to see someone try it—but the more we thought in terms of Mod London, bell bottom pants, jump suits, and rock groups, the more we felt that the concept gave us more problems than it solved. For instance, many of the references in the play are to specific places in 17th Century London that no longer exist; we began to foresee an audience's confusion at a Mrs. Frail in a bell bottom gold lame pants suit talking about going to such and such a pleasure garden. Also, what to do with Sailor Ben, a prototype of a favorite 17th and 18th Century character, the "simple man"? A Royal Navy lieutenant, circa now, just didn't seem right.

After grappling with many details of this kind, we scrapped our original concept and hit on a compromise, one that I think was reasonably successful, and in one area, the incidental music, brilliantly so. Our musical director, Newton Wayland, selected some Bach sonatas and rearranged them for a jazz combo, giving them a syncopated, cool jazz beat. They were wonderfully right and set the tone for the entire production.

For the clothes, I stuck to the silhouette of the period (men: wigs, pyramidal coats, high heels — women: lots of bosom, bustles, fans), but tried to get a contemporary feeling through color. I used very modern neon colors, flat and primary, quite the opposite of the many muted and greyed tones popular in the period.

Colors

I used no patterned fabrics, and stuck to intense, flat areas of color; acid greens, hot pinks, oranges. It was a palette one often sees in modern graphic design, and in a lot of women's clothes today. Also, the kind of juxtapositioning of primaries — greens, purples, reds — one associates with *art nouveau*, another style I felt quite appropriate for "Love for Love" both in terms of its own kind of over-lush decadence and also its current revival.

Mostly I chose chemical colors as opposed to vegetable colors, that is, colors usually associated with chemical dyes instead of vegetable dyes. They're more intense, "fakier," less natural looking. For fabrics, since I was using no pattern detail and hard, bright color, I chose velvets, velveteens, taffetas; fabrics which are made commercially in the colors I wanted, and have the flat intensity of hue I wanted.

As any designer knows, it's very tricky to throw a lot of primary colors together on stage. Reds, purples, oranges

119

and pinks, all splashed together. It's less a problem of course, in dance, or even opera, which are more purely visual and musical experiences. But in the theatre there are words to be heard. What can be a stunning, abstract, kinetic color statement in dance, can be a distraction, or even a downright irritation, in a play.

One or two of the critics felt I fell into this trap in "Love for Love." They found some of the color combinations just a little too psychedelic and jarring for them, or just plain bad taste. One critic made the point that one just doesn't put pink and orange together on the same dress. (He should leaf a bit through "Vogue" or "Harper's Bazaar" these days.)

But it *is* difficult to use a lot of primaries; needless to say, they must be orchestrated much more carefully than neutrals. The color-keying of characters who play together must be meticulously considered.

My instinct, which I think is the instinct of many designers, is to use a fairly neutral palette — the so-called "earth" colors — ochres, umbers, burnt sienna, and olive green, and by launching into such strident primaries in "Love for Love" I *was* going out on a limb.

The last time I designed "Love for Love," a number of years ago, I was very much under the influence of Christian Berard (my single, greatest influence) and my design was extremely muted, almost monochromatic.

Berard was such a genius of the "simple" — not a stroke too many. The most beautiful production I've ever seen was the Jean-Louis Barrault company's production of Moliere's "Scapin," directed by Louis Jouvet and designed by Berard. The palette was limited to variations of grey, with a few accents of rose and orange; it was so simply designed, it dared look "undressed," but it was magnificent.

As for myself, I have such a dislike of excessive detail that I've occasionally risked a production looking too austere. I find often that I cut some detail in my sketches as the clothes are built. I almost never add. Whatever changes occur from the sketch to the finished costume are almost invariably in the taking away.

120

"Love for Love"

Modern neon colors, flat and primary, were used for the pyramidal coat and high heels of Foresight's costume.

I've heard that there are two schools of costume design, the English school and the French school. The English school adores pattern, detail, texture, weight. The French school, perhaps conditioned by couture thinking, or perhaps just because of its superbly rational turn of mind, essentializes to the bone—all is fantastic cutting and draping and a minimum of decorative detail. This is, of course, a generalization, but a fairly accurate one. I would also say, in defense of the English, that no one can mount historical plays, for example the histories of Shakespeare, the way they can, and I personally feel that the French can't touch them when it comes to interpretation of character. Of course, the generalization falls apart completely when one begins to consider some of the great European designers belonging to neither school who combine both elements; the Germans and Czechs and such marvelous Italians as Franco Zeffirelli and Lila di Nobili.

Adaptation of History

To me, the underlying problem in approaching any period play is to take a fresh look at the period in terms of the *play*. Each play is its own world, its own time; each playwright sees his own period, or another, with special eyes. From a design point of view, one cannot, of course, ever be totally historical. Only certain big-budget movie-makers seem to think this is desirable. Good design is basically simplification and selection, and the choices, the selections are determined solely by the playwright's vision. Or rather, the director's and designer's interpretation of that vision, which can, of course, go terribly awry. We chose, through certain means, to give "Love for Love" a rather glossy, brash, contemporary look, which we felt was in keeping with Congreve's glossy, brash, highly sophisticated treatment of *his* contemporaries. I think, visually and certainly in the music, we succeeded in doing what we set out to do. Of course, it was a production not to all tastes, but one always risks that, and what production ever is or can be?

A comparison will show how the approach to a period is completely governed by the play itself. Two productions we've done at the Charles Playhouse had not only the same theatre, the same director and designer, but were both 17th Century satirical comedies. One is "Love for Love" by the Englishman William Congreve, the other is "The Miser" by the Frenchman Moliere, with which we opened *last* season.

Moliere has written a number of decorative commedia pieces ("Scapin" among them), but "The Miser" is not one of them. A later play, even though he wrote it to be a popular success, it stands more in the company of "The Misanthrope" and "Don Juan"—it is darker, more realistic, more a comedy of character. Whereas there's not a real person in "Love for Love," only flashing words, on the other hand Harpagon, the Miser, is a detailed and recognizable man, with dimension and depth.

The atmosphere of "The Miser" is seedy, middle-class, very Paris bourgeois of the late 17th Century. Our set, Harpagon's tatty but once-elegant drawing room (probably in an old hotel around the Place des Vosges), was very real in feeling; stained wood, heavy furniture, dusty hangings. The clothes also were realistic, down to buttons missing from coat sleeves and stains on handkerchiefs. The fabrics were tweeds and heavy wools, real suitings; the palette neutral; bourgeois clothes—believable. The period was essentialized, but realistically, almost cinematically. These were people, in a farce situation to be sure, but also in a room, in a city. In some ways, it was an almost diametrically opposite use of the same exact period for the two plays.

123

The style of a play and the vision of a playwright are, of course, endlessly arguable questions, and approaches to a given play will naturally vary enormously from director to director and designer to designer. Generally, all one can say is that the basic question that faces a designer is to recreate the landscape of the time as seen through each playwright's own peculiar imaginative lens. Sheridan's 18th Century London, is, for example, a far cry from Robert Lowell's 18th Century America, though the period is the same. To show the playwright's inner vision is not always easy, and one can trip and fall quite often, but it's a constantly interesting challenge.

*The search for the innermost charac-
teristic of a period play takes a costume
designer into new areas for inspiration that
often produce lightning bolts of clarifica-
tion. The choice of Frans Hals' paintings
as an inspiration for "The Miser" is as unexpected as it seems apt and appropriate.
That choice instantly focuses in on the reality of living characters — the stolid bour-
geoisie, the burgers of the day — and away
from the more customary stylized courtly
figures borrowed from Boucher or Fra-
gonard. Designer Kurt Wilhelm explains
this choice and outlines his methods of executing the concept with rustic, aged, and
correspondingly real materials.*

*Kurt Wilhelm has been the resident cos-
tume designer at Memphis' Front Street
Theatre, at the Pittsburgh Playhouse, and
at the Atlanta Municipal Theatre. While in
Atlanta, he designed costumes for the
American premiere of "King Arthur" and
for Frank Corsaro's production of "La
Boheme." He is a graduate of the Art
Institute of Chicago and the Goodman
School of Drama. Recently guest designer
at the Penn State Festival Theatre and
Purdue University, he is a member of the
faculty of the University of British Co-
lumbia.*

*The following article first appeared in
"Theatre Crafts," January/February, 1968.*

Stocky Bourgeoisie in "The Miser"

by Kurt Wilhelm

When a designer first approaches Moliere, his mind is filled with visions of frills, lace, and red heels. Excesses of trim flash before his eyes. I was no different. But all these thoughts were erased immediately when the director, Carl Weber, and I first met. His outlook on the play was one of realism, a theatrical realism based on the personality of each character. What this meant was that each character would be dressed according to his means and station in life. The approach was bold, exciting, and rather Teutonic.

We decided on an arbitrary date of 1668 with a feeling that "out-of-date" clothes would be those going back 20 years in style. The Miser, Harpagon, would be at least 15 years behind the times, while his son, Cleante, would be the height of *haute couture*. The clothes would also be "clothes" and not "costumes" and a feeling of age would be apparent everywhere. The stage would be filled with old, worn, real clothes on real people. Even the foppish son would wear clothes that might well be his best but would be far from new. Marianne, the young lady about to be married off to Harpagon, would be in her best clothes but they, too, would be behind the current fashions of the play and have been "washed one hundred times." When we got to the less respectable characters of La Fleche and Frosine, we got down to the real dirt.

Weber felt very strongly about the contrast between the rich and the poor characters. Anselme and his entourage, including dogs and Nubian servants, were straight out of *le roi soleil*, all gold and white, a real *deus ex machina*. They were in sharp contrast to the subdued and rather greyed-down effect that passed before the audience's eyes all evening long. Cleante, who makes his money at the gaming tables, is quite the fop, and was fashionably over-dressed but in keeping with Weber's overall vision; this costume also had to be toned down in the face of the actual look of the period.

Other examples of the contrast we were after were in the costumes of Cleante and his wife, Elise. Unlike her husband she remains at home and wears an old dress that she has outgrown and washed many, many times.

Designers of Moliere plays generally turn to the standard *commedia* characters; to a lesser degree I follow the pack. La Fleche, for example, was loosely based on Brighella. Only certain costumes show this influence. I turned, for the most part, to Daumier and Frans Hals. Daumier for the unsavory "people of the city," Hals for the few elegant people in the play. I always have had a great affection for the stocky, healthy-looking aristocrats of Hals and I tried, in most instances, to create the feeling of the people in these paintings rather than slavishly to reproduce the costumes shown in each painting.

Working with a company over a period of eight months, you can easily think of any actor in terms of the over-all effect of his costume. All the actors in "The Miser," with the exception of three, were members of our resident company. So I was prepared for the fact that Karen Grassle, the actress playing Elise, would need special attention in order to achieve what Weber wanted. On the other hand,

126

Dame Claude   *Jacques*

several of the actors' physical appearances were perfect
for the play. Leon Russom, playing Cleante, had a sturdi-
ness that contrasted wonderfully with the ribbons and
lace helping to make him very attractive to Marianne.
Ruth Maynard, as Frosine, provided a wonderful "big
look" that contrasted with the dainty, girlish detail of her
costume.

I attempted, also, through color, texture, and detail,
to reproduce the feeling of seeing through an aged light,
that is, that particular haze present in the work of Hals
and Daumier that covers and seems to blend trim into
fabric and one layer into another, always unifying but
without monochrome.

In building the costumes, since everything had to look real and old, new problems were presented. I have always enjoyed using strange fabrics. In an effort to reproduce the heavy wools of the period and, at the same time, keep the budget down, I hit on the idea of using blankets for several of the poorer characters in the play. I searched for actual old fabrics with very little success, with the exception of a piece of great old velour curtain in the theatre's scene shop. That I used for Frosine's dress.

With both time and money presenting problems, I decided enough was enough of the search and the fabric would have to be artificially aged. For Frosine's underskirt, I washed and dyed a piece of velveteen that came out looking remarkably similar to actual old fabric. Harpagon needed a coat that once looked grand but that had fallen on bad days. For this, I found a heavy brocade with a perfect wrong side, and after it had been made into his coat, it was subjected to a lot of spraying, dying, and washing. Also, we clipped innumerable threads and this produced a perfect threadbare look.

The household servants were composed of four very shabby, run-down characters. These costumes were built, for the most part, from blankets, homespun, and hopsacking with remnants of braid, livery, or lace in wretched condition decorating them here and there. These characters were played as unsavory bumpkins and the over-all effect was quite funny as they assembled for the party in honor of Marianne and presented their rather disreputable appearances.

I have never quite followed the principles of authentic closings of fastenings for costumes, but I felt with this show the ladies' dresses should lace. This gave the director opportunities for some wonderful business between Elise and Valere to lace and unlace her dress on the way to and from the bedroom.

Another detail that was important to Weber was cold weather. He set the play in winter and wanted a feeling from the set and the costumes that Harpagon had little or no heat, and that everyone was constantly cold. Of course, everyone needed mufflers; so I set the ladies of the theatre's auxiliary, the Dress Circle, to work with their nee-

128

Marianne

Brindavoine

dles. Valere, Elise's lover and gentleman in disguise, wore
two pairs of stockings at once; Elise wore hunting socks
with the feet cut off for gloves; Dame Claude, the housekeeper, wore a blanket as a shawl. Even Cleante had a
muffler which resembled the English school scarves.

The aging seemed to be one of the greater difficulties of
the production. We now were confronted by all these various elements: rich, poor, old, new, blankets, brocades,
velvets, homespun, and lace. Our task was to weave them
into some kind of unified whole. This was done primarily
through color and texture, a great deal of spray, and luck.
Heavy or heavy weave fabrics were used. For the most
part, the colors were in the brown, blue, green range with
some reds, but all greyed-down subtle tones.

All costumes, except those of Cleante and Anselme, which were to stand out, were sprayed or dyed either brown, grey, or both. The effect then was one of obvious contrast between the muted tones and the clear. Cleante's costume was muted through color rather than by means of spray or dye.

Weber was a great taskmaster when it came to details. Bits of ribbon, trim, buttons and missing buttons, or the threads left by missing buttons were discussed at great lengths. It was his attention and patience with details that made the production as realistic as it was. Down to the mother of Marianne who appeared only in a Holbein-like portrait in the curtain call, each character existed as a being living in Paris in 1668.

The production has been labeled "Brechtian," owing to the reality of set, props, and costumes; the use of signs before each act and at the conclusion that stated or commented on the action, and a marvelous throbbing rock'n roll baroque score. I feel, however, that the effect was Moliere with guts.

Sensitivity to one's research into period costumes — that is, good scholarship and an eagle eye — as well as permissiveness in letting the discoveries sometimes lead the design expedition — can produce entirely new effects, characters, and scenes for a play as well as interesting costumes. Patton Campbell's tale about the growth of his period costume designs for a production of "La Traviata" is as detailed and sensitive an exemplar of design methodology as a designer can tell. He recounts the thought process that altered the decade in which the opera is traditionally set; he reveals how the paintings of one artist at the time provided the rich inspiration for not only specific costumes but for an entire event for costumes and setting throughout an Act. By costuming each member of the chorus as a distinct character with a different lifestyle and different mode of dress, he enriched the production in a fresh, new way and at a scale of contribution that few designers attempt.

Patton Campbell was educated at Yale College and Yale Drama School. Among his 50 productions, he designed the picaresque costumes for Broadway's "Man of La Mancha," which he describes elsewhere in this volume. In addition to his designs for the New York City Opera, he has also designed for the Santa Fe Opera, the Central City Opera, Juilliard Opera Theatre, and the Opera Company of Boston. His designs for theatre include "On A Clear

Day You Can See Forever," "The Glass
Menagerie," "After the Fall," and "A Month
in the Country." Among the opera produc-
tions he has designed are "The Makropoulos
Affair," "The Fisherman and His Wife,"
"Cosi Fan Tutti," "Carrie Nation," "Der
Rosenkavalier," "The Pirates of Penzance,"
"The Ballad of Baby Doe," "Capriccio,"
"Wings of the Dove," and more than two
dozen others. He has been on the faculties
of Barnard College, New York University,
and Columbia University.

The following article was first published
in September/October, 1967.

132

The True Vintage of "La Traviata"

by Patton Campbell

When John White, Associate Director of the New York City Opera, asked me to design the costumes for a new production of "La Traviata" at Lincoln Center, I accepted the assignment with delight. All seven operas I had previously costumed for the Company had been either World or New York premieres, and I'd been longing to tackle a great work from the standard repertory. Now I had a warhorse of the operatic world.

I had other reasons for relishing this assignment. In the Broadway theatre, a production is often thrown together in two or three weeks, but I had received my "Traviata" contract seven months before the scheduled opening. For once I could research a project thoroughly, take some time for the sketches, and put the costumes in work early enough to avoid that last minute panic.

Since I had never seen "Traviata," I could approach it almost as if it were a new work. My first task was to listen to a complete recording of the opera. I was struck by the beauty of the entire score—not just by "Sempre Libera" or the tenor's champagne aria, but by the more dramatic scenes as well. But I was dismayed by the thinness of the libretto, with its lack of motivation and wide gaps in the

PATTON CAMPBELL

*The Marquis D'Obigny
(above), wears a
neapolitan costume.
Dancers in the third
act (left), wear moorish
pants of irridescent
blue taffeta with sheer
blouses over dark-
skinned nude leotards.*

plot. It seemed that Piave, Verdi's librettist, assumed everyone was familiar with Dumas *fils'* "Camille." I wasn't. I did, however, remember the Garbo movie, "The Lady of the Camellias," as a very full, dramatic work, so I began to read the novel.

About that time, I was preparing Helen Hayes to tour in "The Circle." In the course of a fitting she told me there had been a real Lady of the Camellias who lived in Paris during the 1840's. Marie Duplessis was her name, and she was the mistress of Dumas *fils*. Next, I discovered two glorious chapters about her in Andre Maurois' biography of the Dumas, "The Titans." There were all the facts: her girlhood as a Norman peasant, her arrival in Paris to become the darling of the *demimonde*, her many love affairs (including a final fling with Liszt), and her death of consumption at the age of twenty-three! There was the famous portrait: almond eyes, white skin, cherry lips, and long black curls. There, too, the actual letter of farewell which survives in the novel, in the play, and in the last act of "Traviata." My initial enthusiasm for the project had become enormous.

Frank Corsaro was hired as director, and the two of us were determined to tell, as honestly as we could, the real story of people who had actually lived. Frank had seemed to some a curious choice for a so-called "romantic" opera. But surely the man who had directed "Hatful of Rain" so sensitively would be right for this story, which, though set in the Romantic Era, is as real as the silver salver that Marie used during her coughing fits. I had no doubts.

I was equally pleased when Patricia Brooks was cast as Violetta. We had been good friends since the endless fitting sessions for her lead in "The Ballad of Baby Doe" and she would make a perfect Violetta. Not only can she sing, she can act. She started as a straight actress. (She met her husband, Theodore Mann, when she went to audition for a bit part in his Circle-In-The-Square Theatre.) Eventually she became a singer, subsidizing her lessons by playing a nun in "The Sound of Music." She has also been a Martha Graham dancer and, to my constant joy, retains a dancer's grace of movement and figure. Few Violettas in history could have played that last scene in a sheer voile nightgown over a body stocking!

135

Pat, Frank, and I formed an informal creative triumvirate for the production. Together we read "The Titans,"
together we read "Camille." And together we went to see
the movie, during its timely revival in Greenwich Village.

Historical Period

"Traviata" has traditionally been performed in contemporary clothes of the 1850's or '60's, the era of the
opera's original success. This is the heyday of the hoop-
skirt. But the idea of hoops seemed to me an intrusion on
the story we were trying to tell. There is something rather
ludicrous about a man trying to embrace a woman with a
steel hoop in his way. And hoops create general acting
difficulties.

Why not move the story back to the time when it really
happened: Paris in the 1840's? I had often heard the '40's
maligned as an ugly transition between the flowery flam-
boyance of the '30's, and the hoopskirted '50's. In the England of Cruikshank, whose illustrations I had followed
closely for "Oliver!," this is certainly true. But over and
over, in costume histories of this period, the beautiful
drawings of Gavarni keep recurring.

Gavarni, christened Guillaume-Sulpice Chevalier (1804–
1866), was the Charles Dana Gibson of the French Romantic Era. Like Gibson, he recorded in ink or wash drawings the beauty, charm and humor of his time. But Gavarni was not content to remain in the salon. He had
Degas' fascination with backstage life, and some of his
most delightful cartoons are of performers in costume, re-
laxing behind the scenes. In Gavarni, I found my natural
ally.

It was he who gave me the solution to my Act III di-
lemma. The City Opera had always let one set of chorus
costumes double for Acts I and III in "Traviata." I wanted
to convince the management to use two sets in the new
production, but I needed a reason more valid than the
passage of time and place indicated in the plot.

In the New York Public Library's Art Reference Room
I came across a photograph of a Gavarni water color called
"Le Bal Masque." The scene is a grand salon, filled with

Violetta Valery's sheer voile nightgown for the fourth act is worn over a body stocking (above). Alfredo Germont's first act costume, (right).

guests in varying degrees of Fancy Dress – and undress: prominent among them is an American Indian stripped to a loin cloth, sporting a goatee, and smoking a big black cigar. I was intrigued, and drove to the Worcester museum to see the original. The museum's curator, I learned, doubted the painting's authenticity, but no matter: it was the kind of scene Gavarni loved to depict; the drawing good, the colors bright and varied. And I had my inspiration for Act III. Flora sings, "The masquers will enliven our revels"; it would be only logical for us to stage *a Bal Masque.*

I found that the amount of source material on Fancy Dress in the 1840's is almost limitless. Victoria and Albert, in their youth, loved to dress up, and undoubtedly encouraged what seems to have been a fad. On nearly every page of fashion plates in "Moniteur da la Mode" and "Petit Courier des Dames," journals of that period, costumes appear alongside ball gowns. (This fact had practical advantages for me; I could accumulate ideas for Acts I and III simultaneously.)

Some of the most delightful aspects of these costumes are their anachronisms. A lady dressed *a la Louis Quinze* wears her *bertha* off the shoulder, just like the contemporary sister beside her; her skirt is not panniered, but rather bell-shaped, supported by a crinoline. During our dress rehearsal a happy accident produced this same kind of comically distorted silhouette. The girl costumed a la chinoise arrived at the ball with her Act I crinoline on under her brocade court robe.

138

A Research Tip

I spent over a month researching the "Traviata" costumes. The amount of source material I assembled was vast, but my job was made easier by a new method of recording fashion plates. A good Polaroid camera with a close-up lens, set on a tripod, records illustrations more quickly and accurately than manual drawing, and more cheaply than photostating. And it reproduces in color. At the New York Public Library, The Metropolitan Museum Costume Institute, and The Museum of the City of New York, the Polaroid was my constant companion. I even took it to The Brooklyn Museum to photograph on dummies actual dresses of the period.

Photographs shuffled like playing cards, books carefully marked, I retired to my studio to begin the actual designing. We had decided to do the production in a subdued, quite limited palette. I had worked within this kind of palette for "Wings of Dove" and was eager to use it again on a larger scale.

History justified our decision. It would not have, if Frank and I had planned a *fin de siecle* setting. At that period the *demimonde* was on the streets; garish Lautrec whores were everywhere. But the *demimondains* of the '40's were creatures of wit, grace, and beauty. Men sought their company to escape the vapid ladies at home who drank vinegar to stay thin, and indulged their morbid phantasies of *la sylphide*. Marie Duplessis had taught herself to read and to play "The Minute Waltz" on the piano.

Final Design

And so, for Act I of a story sad almost from the start, I would use muted mauves, with soft roses and olives. Violetta, I would accent in shell pink. For Act III's Bal Masque, held in the evening and outdoors beneath a pavillion, my colors would range from turquoise through magenta. Violetta would dominate in defiant red Siamese silk, shot with black and embroidered with rubies. In all my final sketches I used tinted water colors to approximate the general tone of Robert Fletcher's sets: beige for Act I, and blue for Act III.

139

I decided not to create a chorus uniform. Members of an opera chorus are chosen primarily for their voices. Physical attributes come second, and these have always varied considerably at the City Opera. In doing "Pinafore" in 1961, I had learned to accept the limitations and, indeed, to capitalize on them. The "sisters, cousins, and aunts" in that production ranged from teenagers to elderly spinsters, and I costumed them to suit their ages. The result was far more effective than dressing them alike ever would have been.

So the *demimondaines* of "Traviata" would dress as individuals. A really fat girl would play a really fat girl, lounging back on a puffy ottoman. An older lady, still in the chorus because "she knows where to enter in Aida," would be the elderly *madame* who advises the *grizettes* breaking into the trade.

In the City Opera chorus is a handsome, statuesque Negro girl, Marie Young. She had been resplendent in yellow and black as the Spanish Ambassador's wife in "Baby Doe" and I wanted to do something special for her in "Traviata." But what? During my research on the 1840's I had come across a lithograph of the great tragedienne Rachel in her favorite role, Roxane in Bejazet. Rachel would have been a natural for Violetta's talented Bohemian circle, and her Roxane costume—exotic, Turkish in derivation—would be magnificent on Marie. Marie would portray Rachel. In Act I she would wear a chic turban with her evening gown, and would attend Flora's ball in Act III still in costume from a performance of "Bejazet." She alone would do the fortune telling at the party (we rejected the usual idiotic practice of having all the chorus girls telling fortunes) while the dancers formed a mystic circle around her.

I refused to succumb to the tradition of putting Act III's *corps de ballet* in banded gypsy skirts, and once again Gavarni rescued me. In the Paris of the '40's, it was the fad for ladies to dress up for *Carnival* in Moorish pants, like dock porters. Gavarni had recorded this in a magazine series called "Les DeBardeurs." There was my inspiration for the girl dancers; they would wear pants of changeable blue taffeta, with sheer blouses over dark-skinned nude leotards.

140

The pants suit, as modish then as it is today, came to my rescue again when, long after the sketches had been completed, another chorus girl was added. "Frank, what can we do?" I asked. "The show is already bid and we're over the budget." He thought a while and then suggested, "Men's costumes usually don't cost as much as women's. What if there were a Lesbian at the ball?" Wonderful. "We'll call her George Sand," I said. "She can make a pass at beautiful Hannah Owen." No sketches were needed. I simply presented the tailor with a copy of a Gavarni drawing I had seen at the Baltimore Museum, and told him to follow it in *aubergine* wool.

My production schedule towards the end was not as lei-
surely as I had originally calculated. I had been asked un-
expectedly to go to Tokyo to costume the first stage production of "Gone With The Wind," and this meant two
weeks away from "Traviata." I left New York after I had
selected the fabrics and returned to three frantic weeks of
fittings and dress rehearsals.

There were the last minute changes. Rosario Galan, the
lead dancer in the *Bal Masque* insisted that I convert her
Goya skirt into a *batta*. I complied. There is no proof that
battas did not exist in the 40's, and Rosario's castanets
dance, with a huge ruffled skirt following her like an angry
serpent, was smashing. The choreographer wanted the
male dancers unmasked: "We can't see their expressions."
No matter. The dance, which seems inane in most productions, came to life when the boys smacked *bandelleros* in
enthusiasm for Rosario.

My one near crisis occurred over the elder Gramont's
costume. In "The Titans," Frank and I had found a marvelous daguerreotype showing corpulent Papa Dumas
snuggling the actress Adah Menken. "That's exactly the
bourgeois look I want for Gramont," said Frank, and I did
the sketch accordingly. Unfortunately, Dominic Cossa,
who had been cast as the elder Gramont, was proud of his
trim figure; the arrival of the stomach pad at his dressing
room evoked a storm that only musical director Julius
Rudel could calm.

We opened on October 23, 1966. In the following day's
"New York Post," Harriet Johnson wrote: "There is a
vintage "La Traviata" at the New York State Theatre. It
arrived last night with so much atmosphere, with so much
mellow wine effervescing with new ideas, it evoked wonder that something so familiar could seem so ecstatically
fresh."

We had succeeded; the warhorse had new life.

141

142

"LA TRAVIATA"

*Choristers in the third act each
wear different costumes*

The much-heralded American premiere of Eugene O'Neill's "More Stately Mansions" took place on September 12, 1967, at the Ahmanson Theatre in Los Angeles. It starred Ingrid Bergman as Deborah, a domineering mother who struggles with her daughter-in-law, Sara, for possession of her son, Simon. Jane Greenwood designed the costumes; her husband, Ben Edwards, designed the sets; Jose Quintero directed. Designer Greenwood's research into American Primitive paintings and New England tombstones and her production arrangements to have the costumes for Ingrid Bergman made in Europe are informative contributions to the craft of costume design.

Born in Liverpool, educated at the Central School of Arts and Crafts in London, Jane Greenwood's first job was as resident designer at the Oxford Playhouse. She stayed there three years, spent the next two seasons cutting costumes at the Stratford Festival, Ontario, and then migrated to New York. She has designed for the Lincoln Center Repertory Company, the American Shakespeare Festival in Stratford, Connecticut, the Metropolitan Opera's National Company, and the National Repertory Theatre. On Broadway she designed "The Ballad of the Sad Cafe" and Sir John Gielgud's production of "Hamlet."

The following interview was published in November/December 1967.

American Primitives for "More Stately Mansions"

an interview with Jane Greenwood

THEATRE CRAFTS: Before we get to the costumes, would you tell us how you got involved with "More Stately Mansions?"

JANE GREENWOOD: I'd worked with Jose Quintero on "La Boheme" and "Susannah and the Elders" for the Metropolitan's National Company. We had a very good relationship working on those two, and he asked me to do this. It's a marvelous play to do. And it's really pioneer territory; none of us saw the Stockholm production. We've read paperbacks of the Stockholm version. Ours will be shorter; a play that runs between three and four hours is too long for today's American audience!

TC: Is this your first O'Neill play?

JG: Yes. That's why it's marvelous to have Jose. There seems to be a special kind of understanding between those two, even though Jose is Panamanian and O'Neill is the most American of American writers. Jose can excite and stimulate you about O'Neill in a way that nobody else can.

TC: You seem to have a special understanding with Jose.

JG: Yes. We have had many, many talks. Serious talks, fun talks, casual talks, picnic talks, studio talks. Rolling the ball, gathering ideas. I find I can't hear him enough during the creative period. I can't emphasize enough how important it is to have a complete understanding between the director and the designer. You all have to work together in a production as a team; if one area shines above another, the balance is wrong. The audience should not come away from the theatre, saying, "what a marvelous actor," or, "what beautiful sets!" The enthusiasm must be overall: what a wonderful evening! And to get this kind of a production, you must have a good director; he has to be firmly in charge.

TC: What about working with O'Neill. Did that . . .

JG: It's extraordinary how engrossed you become with O'Neill. He demands your complete attention to the play. While I was working on the designs I found myself getting —tormented is not the right word, but it's very close—I got very broody and concerned. I've worked on lots of plays, been genuinely involved in them, but I could always get up from my drawing board and forget about what I'd been doing. But O'Neill sticks with you; he drives at you and won't let you go. It was frightening, in a way, but very invigorating. I feel—at least in the initial designs—I've attained in this play a deeper level of designing. I feel there's a certain maturing in my work. I can't exactly explain it to you.

TC: How did you go about developing the costume concept?

JG: O'Neill helps you a great deal. His descriptions of the characters are very clear. Difficult but clear and specific.

TC: Is this why productions of O'Neill are always completely realistic? Why nobody every takes an O'Neill play out of the period he specifies?

JG: He's so evocative of the period he writes in that he

compels you to stick to that period. His people are the people of that time. This play spans the 1830's — 1830 to 1842, to be exact. The women of this period desperately need those soft full skirts and feminine heads; they need that drawing room touch-me-not quality. In the play, when Sara changes into a flamboyant creature who tries to have an affair with her husband, she shocks us. You would lose this if the play were set in the 1920's, when all the women were rather wild. And there's something about the starkness of the men in that period that can't be transferred to another time.

O'Neill's development of Deborah, played by Ingrid Bergman, is absolutely explicit. In her first appearance, she's coming to visit her son whom she hasn't seen in a long while. She's obviously trying to impress him that she's still quite beautiful and womanly, and she's dressed in a style that she hopes will make her attractive to him. In the nicest way — there has to be a charming note. I've used costumes to help the audience register the time changes in the play, but I've dressed Deborah here farther back than 1830. She's wearing something she wore when she was younger, something that represents a look she acquired in her prime. She's in a striped, almost Empire summer coat. She has a leghorn straw hat on. It's designed not only to be flattering, but to suggest that it's late summer and she's making a visit. Women of this period never went outside without a hat, without a certain formality.

In her second appearance, O'Neill tells us she's in her garden and her husband's funeral was that morning. She's completely dressed in white, not black, and she looks much older; her face has a skull-like quality. I have tried to give her the look of a very elegant older woman. She's in a high-necked dress with a lace front. The material is a fine white lawn that they used to use all the time. I couldn't get it here, but I found it in Paris.

147

TC: What sources did you use in researching these costumes?

JC: I went straight to the American primitive painters because they say so much about New England at this period. I used the picture collection at the New York Public Library; you can find anything there. I went to the Gar-

Jane Greenwood's inspiration for Ingrid Bergman's costume as Deborah (above right) was from an American primitive painting of Clarissa Partridge Childs, attributed to Jay Brown.

bish collection in the National Gallery. And I found at the Museum of the City of New York some dolls of this period that had a wonderful sad, used quality appropriate for this play. It never fails to happen when I'm working on a show — a wonderful book came out by Mary Black and Jean Lipman called "American Folk Painting." It showed me real American primitives, with no European influences whatsoever. For a play like this, you must look at real people; you need that kind of solid background to spark you off. I don't mean that you can copy them line for line. At least, I don't work that way. But you must get the feeling of those people.

TC: Can you give a specific example of how you adapted a costume from a painting?

JG: The book had a painting, attributed to Jay Brown, of an older woman, Clarissa Partridge Childs. The front of her dress was an elaborately embroidered front-of-the-bodice with a high collar. She wore a cameo at the neck, and a little ribbon ran underneath the bosom, tying very softly. That gave me the inspiration for Deborah's second dress, the white one. But I designed Deborah's in the style of a later period.

I didn't just use paintings, though. Deborah wears a black dress, in her third appearance, that has a stole and a little cape. The inspiration for the decoration on the stole and cape came from the decoration on New England tombstones. It's a charming, simple design you see over and over again on the tombstones. In researching, you see, you don't always look at costume plates, or people or paintings. You can see something that gives you a mood, a feeling for what you're after, in textiles, in designs on pottery, glass, and china.

149

TC: How did you hit upon tombstones?

JG: I wasn't aware of tombstones at all. I was simply in a bookstore looking for all the available material on New England design, and discovered a book on New England gravestones. You grasp at all the straws; you become insatiable in your search for knowledge about a given period. I suppose I'm a bit of a pedant, but it's better to do too much than too little. It irritates me to see costumes that have been poorly researched, to see superficial details that don't register the period at all.

My husband works very much the same way; we do a lot of research together. We find that working together on a play like this one is very helpful, because we're constantly aware of the overall concept, of the relationship between the scenery and the costumes. I never have any doubts about whether a color will fit into the scenery, because I see the scenery grow. Costumes and scenery develop in complete relationship to each other.

TC: Can you expand on the relationship between the costumes and the scenery in this production?

JG: The scenery, like the costumes, is very specific, very much of the period. There's a starkness, an overall simplicity in the scenery, that's in the play, that's in the mood, and that I've tried to repeat in the costumes. The silhouette of the scenery is strong. The details in it—when they are there—are specific; the details of the summer house in Deborah's garden are architecturally accurate. The trees look like trees in the paintings of the period—they were fond of willows then. My folk art book, incidentally, is being used by the scenery painter.

TC: What is your color scheme for the costumes?

JG: For the men, it's predominantly dark: black, dark blue, and dark green. O'Neill specifies either white or black for Deborah all through the play. For her first appearance I've put her in champagne, but it's so pale that it's hardly a color: it's a neutral. Sara's first in black, then in a nondescript housedress, next blue, then very pale willow-green. But for her last appearance, she wears a purply mauvish silk dress. This not only reflects her flamboyant character, it helps emphasize the tragic elements of the play's ending. She's in purple, Deborah's in white, Simon's in black; the colors give an heroic dimension, an aura of Greek tragedy.

TC: Did you sketch your designs in watercolor, or did you do them in black and white, leaving the color decision until later?

JG: In some plays I feel I need to start out with a quick watercolor sketch to get a feeling of the style. For others,

I feel I have to do a careful, accurate pencil drawing, and color it afterwards. I found that with O'Neill I had to go slowly.

TC: What kinds of materials did you use?

JG: Pure materials. I like to use real materials for period plays. When I say real, I mean real cotton, real silk, real wool. None of the synthetics. There's something about a pure silk, about the way it floats, the way it moves, that you cannot reproduce. And I think the costumes in this play need authentic fabrics; the paintings indicate that the clothes of the period were in the ones I've used.

TC: When did you start working on the costumes? What stage are they at now?

JG: I started in late March, and all the designs are done. Miss Bergman's clothes are already made. As soon as I completed her designs, I flew to Paris to get her approval and discuss how we would get the clothes done. We decided to have them made in Paris by Karinska, who does all those wonderful clothes for the New York City Ballet — her workmanship belongs in museums. Miss Bergman had used her several times, and we wanted to have them made as soon as possible. She wanted the summer free, and she wanted to get the clothes and wig fittings over with before rehearsals. Anyway, Karinska closes down completely in August. So, during that visit, I went to the costume house, met the people concerned with making the clothes, and was rushed around the city to pick fabrics and trimmings. Then I came back to New York only to find that Mme. Karinska was here visiting her mother. Anyway, I had a chance to talk to Mme. Karinska again in New York and discuss with her further how I wanted the costumes to look—the fact that I wanted to keep the silhouette very strong and simple, not let it get too fluffy, out of control. Then I flew back to Paris for the second and third fittings. This time I also conferred with the miliner about the kind of fabric we would use, the number of ruffles and the width of the brim.

I had a slight language problem in Paris but it was rather marvelous. It made me realize that there's a universal understanding of a craft. I'd get hold of a piece of fabric, and do some tiny pleats in it to demonstrate how I wanted a sleeve put in. This visual communication was enough; we had a complete understanding without talking.

TC: What about the wigs?

JG: During my first Paris trip, I flew to London to see Stanley Hall, that brilliant master of wiggery. We had preliminary fittings there, then he flew to Paris for the second fittings. It's very helpful to see the entire silhouette, to compare the wig to the dress and the hat. You get an overall picture of the character.

TC: Where will the rest of the costumes be done?

JG: At Western Costumes in Los Angeles. We thought of using Ray Diffen's firm in New York. He's a superb costume maker, and I love to work with him. But since we're opening in Los Angeles' cultural center, I think it's right that some of the work be done out there.

TC: When you use two companies, is there a possibility that, in the execution, differences in the costumes will show up?

JG: That's what you worry about. That's why it's so important to be very sure of your style, your fabric, and your decoration. You have to be so explicit that nothing can go wrong. I think a designer should follow up a costume while it's being made with tender-loving-care. He must see that the buttons are the right size and shape, that the tucking, even the type of stitch, is right. It sounds a little fine, that kind of meticulous detail, but I think it gives an overall quality that makes for a unified, correct look in a production.

TC: What is the state of your costume budget? With all these real fabrics . . .

JG: When I appear I think the producer goes a little paler underneath his California tan: My Lord, there's that woman with all those expensive clothes. But period plays are expensive by nature of the work that goes into the clothes. People often have the idea that costumes are not well made. That's a fallacy. They're worn about eight times a week. The show may run three years, and they have to withstand constant cleaning, constant quick changes. Costumes have to be much sturdier than the average street clothes.

TC: Was there any pressure on you to use synthetics to keep costs down?

JG: Yes. I've had to be a little firm. If you're going to do an honest job, you can't compromise on the look you want. Western, though, is geared to a film world; their estimates are a little higher than I expected. The movies have more money to spend than we do. But the quality of their workmanship is excellent. Movie clothes get less use, but because of close-ups, the detail on them has to be terribly fine.

TC: What was the most difficult aspect of this production? The coordination problems?

JG: No. The difficult problem was the designing. But it was exciting. From every show you learn something interesting. I wasn't, for example, as aware of the School of American Primitives as I am now. And, of course, I learned a lot from O'Neill himself. With a play like this, you never stop learning.

153

Peter Harvey's comments on the costumes he designed for "Dames at Sea" are extracted from a longer interview about the overall production he designed, which opened at the Bouwerie Lane Theatre on December 15, 1968. Designer Harvey's insight about the task of replacing a costume late in a long run when fabric stocks may have run out, and his comments on critics and their views of costumes are both good lessons about a costume designer's crafts.

Born in Quiriqua, Guatemala, of British colonial pioneer stock, Peter Harvey came to New York in 1959 after living and being educated in Central America, the West Indies, England, Canada, and Florida. His designing assignments for Broadway and Off-Broadway have included "Baby Wants a Kiss" with Joanne Woodward and Paul Newman, "The Boys in the Band," "Sweet Eros," and "The Immoralist." He has also designed for the New York City Ballet—including George Balanchine's "Jewels"—the Metropolitan Opera Ballet, and the Washington National Ballet.

The following interview was first published in "Theatre Crafts" in October, 1969.

Busby Berkeley on a Budget

an interview with Peter Harvey

THEATRE CRAFTS: Peter, how did you happen to get into the project of designing "Dames at Sea" which is such a nostalgic spoof of the Thirties musical?

PETER HARVEY: Jordan Hott, co-producer of "Dames," had seen the Benjamin Britten opera "Noye's Fludde," which I designed some years ago in St. George's Church, so he called me and sent the script. I thought, "Nobody wants to see the Thirties—that's passe now." Of course, it's passe for Off-Off-Broadway—but for Off-Broadway and Broadway the Thirties had just arrived. So the timing worked out well.

TC: What did you aim to achieve for the design of "Dames At Sea"?

PH: The main thing I desired was to retain a coffee-house quality—an Off-Off-Broadway quality of production—even though we were going into a little more elaborate format. I felt the charm of the show was to do it kind of "ricky-ticky"—kind of crummy, but fabulously crummy. I hadn't seen it at the Caffe Cino, but from what I heard, that was what was so really good about it.

TC: What are the design motifs that one uses for the thirties? What did you pick out of old ads or architecture?

PH: It's the futuristic, cubistic, *moderne* style or design that they used then. And the silver, gold, and white we all recognize from the old movies.

TC: A little bit cheap and flashy?

PH: Very. I tried to use the cheapest satin and horrible corrugated cardboard, sprayed with silver paint—everything that was really rather loathsome, but, I hoped, putting it together with as much style as I could.

TC: What's the idea behind this—that you feel the Thirties were really pretty cheezy, awful times?

PH: No, it was kind of an elegant period, really. But again, I was trying to capture the rather Off-Off-Broadway quality of it. In the Theatre of the Ridiculous—I have adored all their productions because they are really just improvisation, and they use stuff they have found in the street—they use flashy, gaudy things with a fantastic boldness in a sort of trashy glamour. It creates a fabulous ambiance that is the part of the Theatre of the Ridiculous I feel is so wonderful. I thought it could be very helpful for this show.

TC: Call it Saturday afternoon in the attic with grandma's trunk?

PH: That's right. That is what it is. The "Dames" costumes we didn't improvise from bits and pieces of other things, though. Perhaps if we had had more time—but you can't find Thirties clothes in the thrift shops any more. So we did make the costumes. I used all of New York's "Fourteenth Street" fabrics—the cheapest satins and very gaudy prints, in vile colors. The Chinese costumes were made of chintz, with a kind of cubistic pattern. It was fortunate that I happened to find it—all terrible fuschia and black and yellow. I put three or four patterns on top of each other, and everything was edged with fuschia sequins. And it was quite marvelous, because it was so impossible. It was quite an effect when the proscenium opened up. Where before, the costumes were black and white and silver, all of a sudden appeared these garish, horrendous colors that were flashing and blinking at you.

Peter Harvey's Thirties-style sailor suits splashed their nostalgia over "Dames at Sea."

TC: Are the sailor suits real, or are those made-up too?

PH: We just went to Army & Navy surplus. There again, wherever I could, I tried to get stuff that was ready-made, that worked, and that looked *cheap*. One problem has come up with the costumes that I don't know how to solve — because some of these garish fabrics were so cheap (like 36 cents a yard); unfortunately they have not retained their colors, and the dry cleaning has faded them out to pastel. So now the show doesn't look quite like I would have it look.

TC: And you can't go back to Fourteenth Street because the bolt is all gone?

PH: Yes. I am sure that the bolt is all gone. Besides, the expense of sewing up a whole new costume isn't cheap.

TC: On a Broadway show, if it looks like it is going to run, do they have a number of costumes already made up? Or do they make up a new costume everytime the old costume wears out or fades?

157

PH: They have understudies for Broadway, and generally complete costumes for the understudies.

TC: With a big show like "Hello Dolly" that is going to be done all over the world (and everyone wants it to look alike in Tokyo, Rome or wherever), doesn't it behoove the designer to be certain that there is going to be access to the kinds of fabrics he wants?

PH: Yes, but materials go out of stock so quickly. I know that Pat Zipprodt, who designed the costumes for "Fiddler on the Roof," has done maybe fourteen companies of "Fiddler," and I know she hasn't been able to get the same patterns and prints and things she used in the original. You just have to go out and try to find the next best thing. Sometimes the whole scheme changes slightly, but you still have the same quality—as has happened in the San Francisco and London productions of "Dames."

Changes

TC: When the actors were rehearsing on the set, were there any problems about their moving on or off stage?

PH: Backstage there were lots of problems, because we had these split-second costume changes and everybody was just tearing off their clothes and putting on new things in back. Meanwhile, stagehands were having to move flats and things in place. And that was time-consuming.

158

TC: Because the pace of the show can't slow down for one second?

PH: No. Absolutely not. That was something that we didn't really plan on. We knew it would be happening, but until there were actors, you couldn't really organize. You can't design shifts beforehand, until you know how many people you will have to shift them. You can design shifts, but when you have to design shifts in conjunction with six actors changing clothes right in the very space where you are shifting scenery, that is rather difficult. That was really the biggest problem with the whole show—getting the space organized and getting people out of each other's way, and just breaking that down into a logical pace. In the beginning, no one thought they could even get into the wedding dresses in time for the finale. Well, we got that going, but still it was always nip-and-tuck. And they always wore the black tap shoes from the other scene, even though it was supposed to be an all-white finale. They never had time to change their shoes. But now that they have been doing it all these months, it is so smooth that they are even changing to white shoes.

Critics and Designers

TC: Do you think, as a side note here, that the designer thinks about the critics as much as the playwright does?

PH: Well, of course, especially in New York, they are very important. But I've had some disappointments with critics, and also some very beautiful notices over the years, and so I've arrived at an in-between feeling. I am happy if I feel that it looks the way I want it to look. And if it is helping the show, and if the director is pleased, then I am content. It really doesn't matter what anybody says if you know yourself that it is right.

TC: Would you say, whether you get good or bad notices, that the reviewers really know what they are talking about? Do you feel that some of the critics are not aware of how much costumes and sets contribute to a show?

PH: I think they are not as aware of it as we would like. But they should not be too aware of all the work that went into such designs; instead they really should just see the finished result and be charmed by it.

159

"Dames" in the Community Theatre

TC: If "Dames" becomes a high school, college and community staple, is there any advice that you would give to designers, costumers, and actors working on it?

PH: Don't get too elaborate—that's the whole thing. Do it with as much style as you can, but don't try to get too elaborate. It should be built economically out of cardboard and ordinary things that one finds around. That seems to let the fabulous Thirties shine through.

Although nearly everyone recognizes how complicated it is to design period costumes, nearly everyone summarily dismisses the design of modern dress costumes as a budgetary expediency or an undesigned shopping chore. Even Actor's Equity is guilty, Pearl Somner chides. Attention to the historical accuracy of style and to the revealing appropriateness of character must be as meticulous in modern dress as for period design. Pearl Somner gives a key to all costume designers when she explains that in reading new scripts she begins by seeing the characters in the nude. Other insights include recognition that shopping is part of the design process and that subtleties in variation and continuity can be achieved in modern dress costumes. Just as Moliere's "Would-Be Gentleman" was surprised to learn that all the while he was speaking prose, Pearl Somner wants would-be costume designers to learn that modern dress costumes must be more than clothes.

After costuming the English production of "Yankee Doodle Comes to Town," designer Somner spent two years with the Berliner Ensemble and a season with the Theatre of the Living Arts in Philadelphia. On Broadway she designed costumes for "The Ninety Day Mistress," and subsequently concentrated on television commercials and industrial films. Her article was first published in "Theatre Crafts" in May/June 1968.

Modern Dress is no Accident

by Pearl Somner

ME: What did you think of the costumes?

HE: (Offhandedly. His mind is somewhere else.) Um . . . fine . . . very . . . nice . . . Yes!

ME: (Here we go again.) Why?

HE: (Taken aback.) Well . . . they didn't bother me.

Who was he? A successful director. Me? A costume designer. And I was let down again. Here was one of the few professional people I thought would not be trapped by the old saw, "If it isn't bad—it must be good."

For my friend, the costumes blended into everything else that was on stage and didn't detract from what he saw. They didn't add, they didn't illuminate character or conform to a unified design; in short, they did not disturb him at all. He really did not see modern dress on stage but merely responded to clothes. And his response was spontaneous and completely subjective.

Even with his long experience in the theatre, his complete and thorough understanding of what goes into a production, he too, was guilty of that major misconception about modern dress plays—that actors wear *clothes* on stage, not *costumes*.

This short-sightedness spells nothing but trouble for a costume designer and worst of all, it dilutes the final production. Unfortunately, it is a short-sightedness that is shared not only by directors but by producers, performers, audiences and, surprisingly, even Actor's Equity.

In textbooks, during pre-production planning and in postmortems, the contributions that costumes make to character and their relevance to the concept of the play must not be sacrificed at any cost. Long hours are spent in detailing the simplest addition to offstage buttons. In practice, if you happen to be a costume designer designing a modern dress play, you might be having conversations like:

ME: But the character would never wear that.

HE: But who'll know? Anyway, it makes
so and so happy.

You go through these sessions knowing that hours and hours will be spent in getting a prop to work properly. Why not the same attention to the details of modern dress costumes?

To producers and business managers a modern dress play represents an economy measure—a meager costume budget. It's simply a matter of beg, borrow, or steal. There are lots and lots of clothes all around and they can pick, choose and juggle outfits until everyone looks *real swell*. And that's why many modern dress shows on Broadway look no better than their summer stock equivalents.

Another wardrobe source can very easily be a performer's own closet. Actor's Equity allows producers to have actors making over $500 supply their own clothes for a modern dress play. In effect, Actor's Equity is also dismissing the pertinence of the costume designer.

If a performer is difficult and if a performer in costume is more difficult, then a performer in modern dress is the most difficult. Again, this is a result of that same short-sightedness. This time, it confuses a performer's image of himself with the character he portrays and traps him into using his off-stage taste in his on-stage clothes.

For me, each costume must express a mood or a feeling for a specific moment or a specific character. Each costume must clarify those elements that make a character unique and separate. These specifics are to be found and used.

If a costume were to hang in limbo, it should evoke a purpose and a meaning. If it were being used by an actress only to look beautiful (hopefully, better than ever), its goal is limited.

When actors are dressed like their audience, there is an additional burden that must be borne by the designer. The audience, aware of what is currently fashionable, sets in motion a series of pressures to lure the designer into presenting costumes as if they were a collection, or to have stars insist that their favorite couturier design for them. Actresses seduced by oohs or ahhs from an audience have a tendency to overdress.

As a costume designer and like everyone else connected with a show, I begin my work by reading the script. For me, however, all the characters are nude. As I begin to understand them and their specific world, their wardrobe slowly gravitates toward each of them. That this wardrobe is modern dress is incidental. For me it is just another aspect of the creative problem.

163

In "The Ninety Day Mistress" on Broadway, I was faced with the problem of dressing three women of the same economic and class milieu living in New York City. Although there is an age difference—a mother, her daughter, and the daughter's friend—there were enough similarities to create a problem in separation and costume identification. In life they could wear each other's clothes with slight modification. However, since costumes should not be interchangeable, I had to design each character's wardrobe. In each wardrobe I had to find a common denominator—in effect, a theme for each character. The themes had to have their own harmonies but orchestrate together.

I decided that my key for each character would be color and that the contemporary silhouette would vary within it.

To find these colors, I went back to the script. It was a comedy, light and gay, and my first requirement was to allow it to determine its own tone. Then I would correlate my palette to it, to enhance its mood, feel, and flow. Warm, clear colors are happy, and their degree of pigment carries an emotional weight. My range became defined.

Leona, the heroine, to be played by Dyan Cannon, was effervescent, fun-loving, possessing candor and strength. The actress's own lion's mane of hair became the sun: her colors would range in this spectrum, lemon through cadmium yellows into orange. Her mother, Judith (Ruth Ford) was eclectic—driving, opinionated, the antagonist and the foil. Her colors would fall short of strident but remain the sharpest complement in the medium scale—pink, aqua, silver, bronze. Phyllis, the friend (Doris Belack) was witty and extroverted, a colorful, garrulous character; she would have the patterns bold and asymmetrical, to support her oblique humor.

I began my research by reading current fashion magazines and trade publications, visiting stores, boutiques, and the Seventh Avenue collections. I hunted for the counterparts of my women characters in what would be their natural environs—Park Avenue, upper Madison Avenue, in galleries and at the Plaza. I looked at them and I listened to them.

Since this was a shopped show rather than a built one, I selected a fashion house in the market that closely approximated my concept. The man with whom I struck an immediate creative harmony was Murray Nieman, the designer for Hannah Troy, Inc. I felt it was necessary that the costumes come from one source because I strongly feel that costumes must have a consistency in design. They must present a singular, strong, unified line. If I used several different sources, I would be destroying the very unity I so purposefully sought. I knew each button, each detail belonged, because they contributed to the costume's unity.

Leona had eight changes during the show. Three were unchangeable because they were locked in by the time of the action or the circumstances of the plot. But in the rest of her wardrobe, I could introduce variety by varying hem lengths, using the textures of different fabrics to give different emotional feelings and, of course, color.

These changes in her wardrobe were to add nuances to her character, provide a visual relief and supply a change of pace. Whether anyone in the audience was affected by all or any of these devices is difficult to know, but they were not accidental. They were as planned and plotted as were the hemlines. Like musicians and painters, a costume designer must employ line, shape, and emotional color.

Sometimes, the audio and the visual aspects of the play work hand in hand. In Judith's second act opening, she discloses the hero's duplicity. She is agitated but her voice maintains traces of a smooth southern accent. What she is doing is fencing, and under her audible words, the text vies with the parry and thrust of her tone and belies a controlled and controlling woman. The script justified something dressy for her to wear, and I was pleased with the opportunity of using a white-silver matelasse for this encounter. The fabric played counterpoint—it shot out glints and glanced its own blows—all very proper and quite fashionable. The intent of the dialogue became visual.

The creation of modern dress on the stage is a difficult creative task. Just as Moliere's "Would Be Gentleman" spoke "prose," everyone in the world wears clothes. To avoid the pressures of so many extraneous influences requires a determined point of view. Modern dress on stage is not a happening—an accident. It is a controlled body of work that has a beginning, a middle, and an end.

*In the new Environmental Theatre, cos-
tumes generally take the form of non-
costumes. That new theatre attempts to
revolutionize the audience's theatre
experiences; therefore, it might more
properly be called Experiential Theatre.
Its costume technique is to underplay the
clothing of the performers — either
figuratively underplay it as anonymous
street clothes, robes, or ponchos, or literally
underplay it as minimal loincloths or
complete nudity. The goal is to make the
audience forget the let's pretend aspect of
theatre performance and see it as real
life. Such costuming of the performers as
non-performers or as mythic everymen can
produce surprisingly subtle effects.*

*The following article first appeared
in a special "Theatre Crafts" issue on
Environmental Theatre, September, 1971.*

166

Covering (and Uncovering)
in Environmental Theatre

by Patricia J. MacKay

Costuming in Environmental Theatre occupies nowhere near the same position it does in more traditional theatre forms. While traditional theatre costuming is often decorative, mood extending, and time-and-place-in-history-orienting, in the environmental theatre, the performers' clothing (or lack of it) is more an extension of the basic concepts that the new theatre form has developed. This new costume is used to bring "realness" to the performance area. It is used to blur divisions between what is life and what is art, as well as to blur distinctions between performer and audience.

The common denominator of the many different people and groups working in environmental theatre is their continual attempt to free the theatre from traditional definitions of roles, places, functions, and uses, which are often firmly rooted in the 19th Century proscenium tradition. For definitions imply lines, categories, barriers, and alienation of the various parts of life.

In order to "break free," environmental theatre often tries to reorient the ways in which an audience sees and experiences. The forms in which this reorientation is presented are varied; but they focus on a simple, "actors' workshop" kind of theatre, on working with actors and texts, often in conjunction. Pared-down, almost non-existent technical craft environments may expose the audience to a totally new way of hearing and perceiving a too-familiar play. Many people also consider the electronic, multimedia theatre, which reorients by light and sound, to be environmental. Richard Schechner, while editor of "The Drama Review," proved himself to be Boswell of the movement, of which he also is a practitioner, and in the Spring 1968 issue of "TDR" he defined and named this trend "Environmental Theatre." Since then that phrase has become an ambiguous catch-all for many people, yet it does not really focus in on the myriad aspects of the movement. The phrase "experiential" theatre may prove to be a clearer, more accurate, and more finely honed term for the movement.

However, "environmental" does have the advantage that by its very ambiguity it can be as all inclusive as the many varied works that are generally described as environmental theatre.

Schechner further refined his definitions at a Spring 1971 meeting of New York's Drama Desk, where he pointed out what had become clear about the movement: that is, that it aims for a blurring of the distinction between stage and house, between performance and real life, between rehearsal and performance, audience and actors, and between the play as a fixed or a living thing.

Choreographer-dancer Ann Halprin, in the Spring-Summer 1968 issue of "Arts and Society," commented on the kind of theatre that interested her: "A theatre where everything is experienced as if for the first time, a theatre of risk, spontaniety, exposure, and intensity. I want a partnership of the audience and the performer. I have stripped away all ties with conventional dance forms: the lives of the individual performers, the training, rehearsals, and the performances for a process in itself is the experience. . . . I wish to extend every kind of perception.

Nudity is the extreme of environmental theatre's efforts to break through traditional costume concepts. This kind of non-costume, as in the Firehouse Theatre's "Faust" (below) has a blunt directness that many audiences find disconcerting.

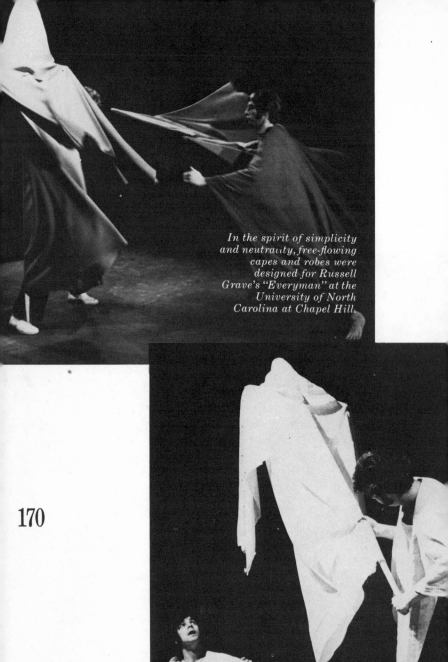

In the spirit of simplicity and neutrality, free-flowing capes and robes were designed for Russell Grave's "Everyman" at the University of North Carolina at Chapel Hill.

170

I want to participate in events of supreme authenticity, to involve people with their environment so that life is lived whole."

Jerry Rojo, designer of the spaces for, among others, the Performance Group's "Macbeth" and "Commune," is far more simple in his definition: "One of the things that environmental theatre is trying to suggest is that theatre should not have conventions—that no art form should have conventions."

What has been happening in this environmental theatre since the late 1960's cannot be considered outside of the context of the revolution throughout our society. Broader than a political movement, the revolution we have witnessed during the past several years is also one of the mind. Political targets, methods, and motivations have certainly been part of the revolutionary activity. But, principally it has encouraged the overthrow of older, established, traditional, stereotyped structures of thought. Styles of dressing, places and ways of living, patterns of consumer consumption, corporate and governmental infallibility have all been called into question and have, in many instances been redefined. Similarly, traditional theatre has been called into question.

Naturally, there is no single consistent approach used over-all for environmental theatre costumes: rather, several approaches reinforce the variations in environmental theatre itself. They span from the essential reality, honesty, and shock value of nudity to the electronic, intermedia totality of Alwin Nikolais' projected costume designs. Along the way, environmental theatre costumers also use found objects (the way their stage designers use found spaces). They may take their search for honesty in "facing the body" just as far as a simple loincloth, or they may use every day street clothing so as to make no distinction between actors and audience. In this vein also, clothing fades into oblivion.

Nudity is perhaps the most publicized aspect of environmental theatre. Far from being licentious when practiced by the groups who are seriously *into* theatre (not merely "seeking commercial fame and fortune" and therefore exploitive), this form of non-costume takes on an honesty

171

Designers Eugene and Franne Lee created the costumes and environments in which Andre Gregory's Manhattan Project plays its remarkably moving and hilarious "Alice in Wonderland." Franne Lee used second hand rosettes for a vest worn by The Red Queen (above) and old quilts for The Dirigible Prince (below).

in keeping with the work as a whole. The Beck's Living Theatre, The Performance Group's "Dionysius in '69," and Tom O'Horgan's "Hair" have all been well exposed. A production of "Faust" by the Firehouse Theatre is also similarly stripped. Douglas Dyer, creator of "Stomp," points out that when his group put that production on at New York's Public Theatre, nudity, which had not been an element at the University of Texas, was added. He comments, "There was that truth and honesty about nudity that also comes with confession or a technique of telling the truth about yourself. All of these things contribute very much to the environmental theatre trend."

The question that as yet remains unanswered (and maybe always will) is: did their honesty about the body achieve its goal? Did it succeed in making audiences more aware of the environments of their minds, of the physical enclosures they move through every day? Or, was it ultimately an ego trip for the actors, directors, and designers who found nudity to be the end of their search for confronting reality and breaking the traditions – not only of theatre, but also society?

Bare essential costuming (with the accent less on the bare) is the next step from nudity. Loincloths, like those used by Poland's Jerzy Grotowski in "The Constant Prince," or simple leotards and tights cover the performer's body but are so neutrally minimal as to be a negative statement. Although some audiences even find loincloths unnerving, most designers feel that these neutral costumes fade away, freeing the audience's attention to focus elsewhere.

173

Sally Jacobs' colorful tunics or robes for Peter Brook's stripped production of "A Midsummer Night's Dream" were simple, uniform-like sheaths, but they were still rather more in the "designed" tradition than in the new anonymity.

"Life Rite," a work developed at Bowling Green State University by John Scott, playwright in residence, and student director Philip Schenk, makes a more neutral statement in its uniform poncho costuming. As Scott writes about the concept for "Life Rite," "Ritual suggests, and is, basic, raw, unaffected experience. The magic of the rite is its capacity to group many participants without extensive use of artificial stimulae. The action must be simple. The content must be basic enough to crush intellectual and emotional barriers. In production these principles were honored."

Thus the costuming for this production was limited to simple ponchos. Not only is this the kind of clothing that is ideal for groups in college, universities, and elsewhere with low budgets — because construction is simply a matter of selecting material and sewing seams — but its simplicity contributes to the overall effect of the work.

The value of this negative neutrality was also explored by Russell Graves in his production of "Everyman" at the University of North Carolina at Chapel Hill. About the costuming Graves writes: "The basic point of departure for design of the costumes was one of simple neutrality of statement, fulfilled by a poncho-like covering over tights. It was a simple costume in conception, but the final design was the result of a great deal of experimentation to find the material and pattern that would lend themselves to the greatest number of movement effects.

"Departures from this basic design were made only for very special purposes (e.g. the narrator, Everyman, and the monk). The basic costume was integrated into the conception of the production by relating it to the character of Everyman himself. He was sometimes dressed in it and at other times wore only a breechclout."

174 Similarly, the use of every day street clothing as costuming is both a neutral statement and a confrontation with "reality." Its often across-the-board use breaks through a number of traditional barriers and raises questions about the relation of "life" and "art" — their separateness or togetherness. Since many of the works are contemporary in theme, it seems more or less natural that street clothing should be used. But in other productions, street clothing is used where "period pieces" have been worn in the past. Of course, modern dress productions of Shakespeare's "Hamlet" and "Julius Caesar" long ago set an historical precedent for works like the Performance Group's "Macbeth" and the student productions of Ibsen and Brecht's "Baal" designed by George Lindsay at the Loeb Center in Cambridge.

Easily constructed ponchos made neutral costumes for the performers of John Scott's "Life Rite" (left) at Ohio's Bowling Green University. Simple tunics in colorful satins designed by Sally Jacob for Peter Brook's "Midsummer Night's Dream" (below) are other examples of the new theatre's quest for neutral costumes.

However, within the context of this entire tradition-barrier-breaking theatre, the use of street clothing begins to take on some new aspects. It forces one to question if there really is any sacred barrier between what a performer wears every day and what he puts on to perform. . . . Can we, in terms of this new theatre, draw the line (and if so, where?) between what is the beginning and the end of his performance and therefore the point at which the performer would put on or take off his "costume"?

Further, in terms of the audience, they are brought into confrontation with another bit of their everyday environment and forced to question the role it plays. Can we assure that what one wears every day is simply functional clothing, or is it much more a costume for the roles one assumes in life? It is precisely the crossing of this kind of barrier and the bringing together of formerly categorized elements of life that the environmental theatre strives for.

In the Performance Group's "Commune" there is a breakdown between what is the actors' clothing and what is the audience's. Demonstrating the Christian-Marxist-Communal doctrine that "what is mine is yours," the actors go among the audience collecting clothing, asking "give to the poor," and "share, share." A jacket, shirt, tie, scarf and a wristwatch are taken by the performers to add to their own "costumes." The audience then strongly feels its individual reactions of generosity or protective possessiveness—reactions that reinforce the performers' attempts to break through the costume distinction.

176

Although some might consider street clothing in the same category as found objects, Franne Newman Lee, wife and designer partner of Eugene Lee, suggests that the most characteristic element of all costume work for environmental theatre is its element of reality. She points out that while her costuming for Andre Gregory's Manhattan Project, "Alice in Wonderland" is not "realistic," it uses "real" elements. She has taken second hand quilts, jackets, hats, and dresses (all objects which had a former life, another reality) and transformed them into clothing for the Mad Hatter, the Dirigible Prince, and the Red Queen, and other Lewis Carroll creatures.

Beyond found clothes and street clothes and at the other end of the scale from nudity, are the costumes of Alwin Nikolais. The electronic totality of his work is considered by many people to be environmental. In many ways his designs for a dance theatre piece like "Tent" are the most *together* that has been done. He has managed to destroy, at least visually, the lines which separate dance actions from costume and environmental set. In addition, his use of projected lighting patterns in this and other works creates costume fabric patterns and raises questions about the ambiguity or identity of costume, set, dancer, and lighting.

While costuming is not the focal point of the environmental theatre, it does extend and exhibit the tenets held by the practitioners of this new theatre approach. The future of costuming? Will there be a return to beautifully designed clothing? It hardly seems likely within the context of the environmental theatre. Yet, at the same time, it would not appear that total nudity is the direction in which environmental theatre is traveling; for in order to serve this theatre, it must have the shock value of realism, which is a commodity easily lost by overexposure. It appears more likely, as increasing numbers of people are beginning to think of their everyday street dress as costume—something outlandishly ethnic or serviceably workmanlike—that whatever distinctions of dress between the audience and the performer now remain, will disappear if environmental theatre designers have their way.

177

As in his minutely detailed narrative on designing costumes for "La Traviata," Patton Campbell briefly sketches the same process for the costume designs in "Man of La Mancha." The repetition of his methodology, as directed toward a different historical period, reconfirms several significant steps — selection of an appropriate, lesser-known artist as inspiration, and selection of designs, colors, and materials for individual costumes. For this production, the technique of aging the costumes without decreasing their durability was a special task. Horse heads and armor were also special design requirements which, in the mirror scene, are turned into a glittering spectacle. In that scene, Cervantes' son-in-law comes to him dressed as a black knight to make him see his Don Quixote guise for the mad posturing it is. The breastplate of the black knight is encrusted with a mosaic of mirrors that catch the light. When mirrored shields are held up to Cervantes so that he (and the audience) can see reality, the light dances off the mirrored mosaic breastplate and off ball mirrors in the ceiling, reflecting onto the audience and the walls of the darkened auditorium like a planetarium's stars flashing in the night. Don Quixote — and the audience — crumbles before this brilliant bit of costuming symbolism.

For Patton Campbell's biographical sketch see page 131. The following article was first published in "Theatre Crafts" in May/June, 1967.

179

Stylized Rustics in "Man of La Mancha"

by Patton Campbell

"Man of La Mancha" ran for several successful years at New York's ANTA Washington Square Theatre and then moved to Broadway. The National Company, headed by Jose Ferrer, had theatre-goers clamoring for tickets up and down the Eastern Seaboard, and a West Coast Company, headed by Richard Kiley, who was our original Don Quixote, opened in Los Angeles and trouped eastward. In retrospect this seems an amazing response to a production that in its inception in the summer of 1965 at the gingerbread Goodspeed Opera House on the Connecticut River, seemed to be no more than an intriguing idea, and surely not the critical and commercial success it has turned out to be.

My involvement with "Man of La Mancha" began when Howard Bay asked me if I'd be available to work with him on the costumes. At that time I was designing and executing New England attic clothes for Jack Beeson's opera "Lizzie Borden." My first reading of Dale Wasserman's script seemed to offer a challenge, especially since I had to switch my thinking from the realism of Fall River in the 1880's, to a play-within-a-play set in Spain during the Inquisition. From subsequent readings, a sketchy list of the play's requirements evolved, and special considerations such as fast *a vista* changes, horses, armor, and costume props were noted. Our imaginations were further whetted when we heard Joe Darion's lyrics croaked like a bullfrog by the composer Mitch Leigh.

We met with the director, Albert Marre, to discuss his approach to the production from both the emotional and practical points of view. We all agreed that the clothes worn by the Inquisition prisoners should be as real as possible, but that there could be a greater degree of stylization when Cervantes and his fellow inmates step into Cervantes' improvised play. We would be justified to use suggestion rather than accurate delineation because in the very first prison scene Cervantes asks the audience to participate in an entertainment. That way Quixote's upstage, offstage bout with the windmill could be suggested by using sound effects combined with shadows that appeared to be of the windmill's circulating blades. So, too, the horse and donkey could be suggested by makeshift sawhorses hauled along by prisoner-actors wearing crude animal heads. Such masks might have found their way into Cervantes' prop trunk from some indigent *commedia* troupe. Just as the audience is fascinated watching Cervantes make-up for his role as Don Quixote, so too, they might enjoy seeing a band of gypsies they easily recognize as the muleteers, dressed in funny robes and homemade turbans.

181

In search of visual inspiration for our designs, we began with Doré. After all, his illustrations for the novel are the most familiar, and the audience might have some pleasure in recognizing them. Although filled with Victorian anachronisms, they have the spirit and grotesque humor of the story. Unfortunately, the amount of source material available for low-life characters in period productions seems to be in inverse proportion to the distance back in time. With the exception of Rembrandt, the great painters in history portrayed mostly noble lords and ladies

and rarely beggars and whores. It was easy to find ideas for Corrasco and for Quixote's niece in the works of Velasquez, but to dress the muleteers in a variety of rustic forms proved more difficult. I was fortunate to find in the New York Public Library a colored reproduction of a German artist's sketchbook. The artist, Christoph Weiditz, had visited Spain in the sixteenth century and had recorded in naive and charming drawings the manners and dress of peasants at work and in play. This sketchbook became an invaluable source and one of the drawings provided the spirit, if not the actual choreography, for Jack Cole's gypsy dance.

Early in our planning, Howard Bay and I agreed that a considerable variation of crude textures would give our production the look we wanted. Aldonza's costume, for instance, began with the idea of a cowhide doublet given as pawn for her services by one of the muleteers. To this she adds a token blouse of knotted fishnet to reveal as much as possible of her commodity. Her skirt is a ragged hunk of coarsely woven "wool." And, of course, nothing makes as beautiful rags as handwoven Indian tussah, the raw silk at $15 a yard.

Once the actual forms were decided on, we began looking for samples of leather, fur, and textured wools to make the basques, doublets, and breeches. Our search took us to the outlet shops on West 40th Street, downtown as far as Orchard Street and back again to Dazian's theatrical emporium. We were surprised to find there, a whole line of rought-looking weaves of durable cotton and synthetic casement cloths and upholstery fabrics in an interesting range of muted colors. We had decided on a grey palette for the prison scene. For the inn scene we used variations of earth colors enhanced by dull greens, with the dominant accent being the burnt orange of Aldonza's skirt. Cool, cerebral colors were chosen for the hypocritical family of Quixote: blue-gray for the padre, dark blue for the housekeeper, with the blue and green checked pattern of the niece predominating. The only seemingly elegant fabrics in the production are the black and green, changeable taffeta used for the Duke Corrasco's costume and its ribbing and panes of black velvet. Our palette was purposely

183

184

The sketchbook of
Christoph Weiditz,
(above), a German
artist who visited
Spain in the Sixteenth
Century, provided
designer Patton
Campbell with an
inspiration for
costuming the gypsies
and muleteers as well
as Sancho Panza and
Don Quixote (right and
facing page top).

muted, but brightened briefly by the appearance of the gypsies. For them we used Moorish patterns of felt, in full intensities, appliqued to coarsely-woven, bright, nubby wool tweeds.

Sketches approved and fabrics chosen, drapers then made muslin mock-ups of our designs. Details of dagging and slashing were penciled on the patterns and the actors were called from rehearsal to check for fit and mobility. After the first fitting, each pattern was cut of the actual fabric to be used and the costume stitched for a final check. The last step was that of "breaking down." This is often perplexing to those who have worked so hard to make a new costume of strength and beauty. Why can't just any old costume be used to simulate rags? Because an old costume would not necessarily satisfy the design requirements, and mostly because actual old clothes could never withstand the rigors of eight performances a week.

For "Man of La Mancha" almost all the costumes were frayed with scissors, roughed up with a wire brush, dumped into tubs of dirty water, sprayed and splotched with analine dye solutions, and hung up on nails, never to be pressed again. The wardrobe woman's principal task in maintaining the production was to keep the costume aged and dirty looking, yet fresh and sweet-smelling to wear.

Among the special effects the production required were the horse and donkey heads. In their execution they underwent several metamorphoses. We molded merry-go-round heads in plastic, then the molds were made-up with paint, and rope manes were added. At Goodspeed the heads proved neither funny nor, more importantly, light enough for the dancers when Jack Cole's vigorous choreography was added. In our next attempt we wired buckram with the comic exaggerations of Howard Bay's sketches molded in. These masks were light, porous enough for breathing, but sadly uncomfortable when the actors had to nap at the edge of the wall. The final solution was molded latex. It proved to be both light enough and flexible enough to fill all our needs.

The armor we needed was molded in durable plastic, using an actual suit of the period as our model. The molds were spray-painted to give them the appearance of metal.

The Knight-of-the-Mirrors and the shields carried by his attendants were decorated with mosaics made from sheets of plastic mirror. This was cut easily with shears that also edged the mirrors so the actors could gesture freely without the fear of bloody fingers. The Knight's armor was processed further to appear battered and ancient. During the first dress rehearsals in New York, we discovered that Richard Kiley was very uncomfortable in his plastic breastplate, especially when he had to roll all the way down to the apron from upstage after the windmill episode. We remade his armor in leather. Embellished with rope and painted, it simulated the original and solved the problem.

The basic problem in costuming Quixote was our having to transform Kiley's well-proportioned, football-player physique into that of a stooped, stringy, elderly knight. (When we first worked together in "Redhead," our problem had been just the opposite. At that time he was playing a London music hall strongman.) The vertical line had to be emphasized wherever possible: a slight hump was added to his back, his shoulders were set in and heightened, the torso was cut long, and his breeches slopped down far enough to obscure his muscular calves. This same elongation of the figure was used for his successors Jose Ferrer and John Cullum.

The success of a costume designer is largely measured by the degree to which he has aided the performers in realizing their characterizations. This had been our aim from the first reading of the script.

187

When no pictorial documentation or precedent for the costumes of a period exist — as for prehistoric ages, mythical times, or the future — a costume designer must do a kind of let's-pretend detective work among imaginary clues. His success depends on the precision of his inventiveness and on insatiable curiosity. To find the atmosphere of the costumes for "Two By Two," the musical with Danny Kaye that opened in November of 1970 at the Imperial Theatre on Broadway, Fred Voelpel reconstructed the sociological background of Noah's life before the Flood. He asked his imaginary witnesses about life-styles then and about tailors at that time. It was an intellectual process, but if it can produce as richly alive a wardrobe as it did in designer Voelpel's hands, it is an imaginary research process that other designers can well investigate.

Fred Voelpel has created costumes and sets for theatre and television productions since 1956, and in 1970 he won the New York Critics Award for "The Effect of Gamma Rays on Man-in-the-Moon Marigolds." He earned the same award in 1962 for "No Strings," which also garnered him a Tony nomination. He is active with the O'Neill Theatre Center, its annual Playwright's Conference, Critic's Institute, and the National Theatre of the Deaf. "Two By Two" was his third production for Richard Rodgers. The following article first appeared in January/February 1971.

Antediluvian Handcrafts
for "Two By Two"

an interview with Fred Voelpel

"Two By Two," Richard Rodgers' new musical, is based on Clifford Odets' play, "The Flowering Peach," but it is substantially different. The original play was predicated on a retelling of the Noah story in the vernacular of the Upper West Side and the boroughs of New York City. Much of that syntax and rhythm has been retained, and has gone into the musical numbers, and a lot of it has disappeared completely.

189

As a designer, it seems to have been my lot to have worked on a number of shows that are set in curious periods of history. For example, I did the costumes for the Lincoln Center production of "Tiger at the Gates." It was not the conventional Greek or Trojan look. We really do not know what they looked like because that is the period that mythology is based on. We have pictures of artists' interpretations of what things were, but any artist bends a subject to his own purpose. So we are seeing periods through several sets of eyes. Also, I have designed several other Babylonian, Assyrian, and similar period shows.

Antediluvian handcrafts set the fashion for Noah, played by Danny Kaye, and his family (above).

In addition, I will be very honest. "Oh! Calcutta!" helped a lot, because you get down to what movement and physical behaviour is all about when people are nearly naked. Clothes can be looked at in many different ways, and being decorative and attractive is just part of it all.

"Two By Two" is really based on the pre-history civilization of Ur—like that of Sumer it was centered in lower Persia. That civilization is so early that almost nothing is documented, and Noah makes a great deal in the show of writing the Bible. It is a very funny show—which is one of its strong points. Some of the other themes running through the play are centered around family relationships; understanding established concepts as opposed to new ideas; the ability to start over—a fascinating concept that all dream about. Also, there is conflict in the youngest son, who disagrees violently with what God tells him. "Two By Two" also brings up the beginnings of our ideas about what God is, and what we do when God fails us.

Design Period

The first job of a costume designer is to put yourself in the period. But you must also constantly remember, in this case, that it is a Richard Rodger's musical for an audience in 1971. You must never lose sight of that because many of the things that could be designed for a production like this would look good in a museum but might not mean anything to the audience.

First you analyze where the people are in civilization and how sophisticated they are. In this case, the people in "Two By Two" are nomads. They live in a rubble heap, and have to be very inventive about whatever they put on. They have to make it themselves out of whatever they are able to scrounge. Because these people are poor, there are very few costumes for the eight actors. In addition, the clothes they do have become tablecloths, bundles, bandages, and towels; they turn their clothes into anything that will protect them from the weather.

Further, they make the clothes themselves and do not have hours to spend making beautiful things—these people are more serious about the utilitarian. Historically, we know that people of this period would have only what they could weave themselves, or what they could take from animals. Thus, in order to make costume decisions for "Two By Two," we analyzed what they could have physically made under those conditions.

Handmade Look

As a designer you put yourself in that situation; in other words, you say "If I were living then, what could I make?" We have taken the position that Noah's wife, Esther, made their clothing out of goat's hair, string, hemp, and grass.

My job for the theatre at this point is to create the illusion that that is indeed what they did. Certainly, we had to use existing cloth, but we have broken it down into the smallest components. To convey the handmade look, we are using strips of cloth. Each strip is being rewoven into a design as if it were a small piece of patchwork quilt. Then these loose, open strips of material are tied together again to form garments. It is a very organic, intellectual wardrobe.

Antique Colors

There is a palette of antique colors—certain blues people made by grinding stones, and certain reds that come from shellfish. In addition, the clothing of Noah's family has been beaten by the sun, the rain, and sand. Thus the garments appear grey and beige.

In addition, there was another element of this production which had to be taken into consideration when choosing costume colors. All the animals, all the references to God, all the elements that we do not choose to show on stage are indicated, or referred to, by subliminal projections which wash across the entire stage—including the set.

The set is very tactile—boards, lumber, crude rocks, and rubble. Noah's family dismantles their house all through the first act in order to build the ark. By the time that act ends there is virtually nothing left on stage except rocks. The ark of the second act is made of elements we saw in the first act. However, in order to support the projections

Handcrafted details of fur and fabric (top, left), of loosely woven strips (top, right), and of fringed, rewoven squares (left) created the materials for Noah's nomadic family. Noah's costume (below) and Fred Voelpel's sketch of it (below, left) showed a reverse aging as God turned Noah into a younger man in preparation for the flood.

(famous paintings of God, the animals, etc.) the set has to be very bland. It must act as a screen, so the set has been painted in subtle ways—actually more subtle than if you were doing it without projections.

Therefore the colors of the clothes cannot be much more brilliant than they are or it will look out of balance with the set. I find it is true that quite often you get a very strong idea and then all the other elements in a production do what they can to tear away at it. As a designer you have to try to preserve as much as you can of the big idea, keeping all the other elements in balance.

Materials and Weaving

Once I decided how the fabric should look—handwoven and weathered, I purchased material which had that feeling. Materials for the costumes include: leathers, suedes, all kinds of hemp and jute, yarns and complicated braids. One of our problems was with metallics. The story is really set in the Bronze Age so it is wrong to use the kinds of sequins, beads, and jewelry that might be associated with a Broadway musical.

In working the patterns into the strips of cloth to create the handwoven look, we used simple geometric patterns, nothing off center, nothing with a beautiful curve. Our patterns have to look naive since our characters are unsophisticated. (If I could have had 10-year-old children to do the weaving, I would have been happy because they design in squares, circles, and diamonds. They don't see the more complicated patterns and arabesque shapes that a more sophisticated person does.)

194

The end result gives the handwoven illusion that I wanted. It looks as if someone sat down and created patterns on each strip (as indeed the women working at the costume shop did do) and then when the strips were finished, they were pieced together to make a garment. For groups outside of the professional theatre, doing this show would not be difficult because the costume is made up of little pieces. Many theatres have costumes already, that can be taken apart and used in small ways as we are doing here. They don't have to be made on a big cutting table with dress forms; and we have done very little fitting of the costumes in the traditional sense.

*Flower child Japheth (top, left) and businessman Shem
(sketch and photo, middle left and right) were costumed in
fabric squares that gave a handwoven look. Metallic colors and
fabrics were used to set apart the character Golde
(top, right) from members of Noah's family.*

Scene By Scene

In "Two By Two," there is no way of lining up the drawings in an orderly scene by scene sequence. In other
shows that can be done and a designer can see exactly
what it will look like. You can break it down; for example,

the star enters wearing street clothes and a fur and then changes to a peignoir. But that cannot be done for this show because the characters sleep, cook, eat, and travel in their clothing. You have to find the right way to wear the costumes for each scene as you go along during rehearsals and preview.

The reason for this approach is that we only have eight basic costumes which are used and worn many different ways. These eight costumes can be used so that we will get about 64 different costumes and/or props. The actor is important in the costuming for "Two By Two" because many of the shapes (and, in fact, the success of the idea) are dependent on how successfully the actor can relate the wrap to himself, and make it seem natural. This approach leaves much more imagination for the actor and it inhibits him less, but it puts a burden on him to respond to the many ways the costume can be worn. Our actors are excited about being able to invent as they go along.

Stylistically, the basic silhouette of the costumes comes from the Ur Civilization; and, of course, the garments reflect and project the characters in the play. Danny Kaye as Noah is the pivotal character. Since he is on stage a large percentage of the time, there is an element in his costume which relates to all the other garments. Each of Noah and Esther's sons and their wives have very specific personalities. The oldest son, Shem, is the businessman — the herder and the person who sells land. His wife, Leah, is just a little aggressive so her costume colors are a little shriller and stronger than the others. The second couple, Ham and Rachel, are a mismatched couple and that too comes out in their costuming. The wife is actually attracted to the youngest son — Japhet, who is almost like a flower child. For his garments I have used violets, and soft, brownish calf colors. Ham is very vain, self-centered, and has a roving eye. He is, in fact, interested in Goldie. Goldie is an acolyte from an existing temple and the one person in the play from outside the family group — as such she is quite bizarre looking.

If we could have all the actors working barefoot, it would be terrific, but since our leading actor has to wear

196

specially designed sandals, it only stands to reason that a few other people in the cast must also wear sandals so there will be a balance. The people in "Two By Two" are specific characters — not just a chorus — so each shoe has to be thought out carefully.

In a sense, I have a shoe fetish. I am very careful about shoes and spend a great deal of time choosing them. However, for a period show, to go down the road of exquisitely made period shoes is the kind of expense that is not necessary to incur unless you have a very comfortable budget, or a star with certain demands.

I do sketches of the kinds of shoes that would be ideal for a part, and usually hire an assistant to go out and find something comparable on the market. My feeling is that the market is very good for shoe buying, if you research it.

Of course, the ideal way would be to have them all made, the way the Europeans do it. They have careful, intelligent craftsmen who understand, but, here the theatrical dance shoe business is in trouble because very few companies will even discuss making shoes for dancers — many of them are more interested in selling shoes to the general public. Every show has problems with shoes because there is a lack of craftsmen to make them within a reasonable time for a reasonable amount of money.

Craftsmanship in this country is in terrible shape. Many parts of the theatre industry are in trouble too. Too many people coming into the theatre think that the only job is performing. Too many schools are overly slanted towards performing and no industry can absorb that number of college graduates. Many students are not aware of the large numbers of other jobs available in the theatre that do not involve performing.

197

In the long run, who is to say that an evening in the theatre now involves any kind of experience that we have been trained to do. Maybe it is becoming a whole other kind of entertainment. Too many students coming into the theatre want only to do what has been done before.

There is a real need for people who are getting into the crafts of the theatre — who want to make theatre.

Virtually without precedent is costume design for abstract, mythological, almost geological characters such as those in Aeschylus' "Prometheus Bound." Douglas Russell's research and design process for a production of that super-human work at the Stanford Repertory Theatre's inaugural 1965–66 season ultimately led him to mineralogy, that most ancient trove of mythic fossils, and to the abstractions of its rock crystals. This powerful imagery had to yield somewhat in the final designs, however, so that the non-human costumes could be tempered to the actors' movement and the characters would not all be equally or literally bound.

Douglas A. Russell, the costume designer for the Stanford Repertory Theatre, has also designed 56 productions for the Oregon Shakespeare Festival at Ashland. He designed "Twelfth Night" for the Actor's Workshop, "Henry VIII" and "Measure for Measure" for the National Shakespeare Festival at San Diego, and "Misalliance" and "Twelfth Night" for the American Conservatory Theatre. He is Associate Professor of Costume Design and Art History in Stanford's Drama Department, and has taught in the past at the Carnegie Institute of Technology, the University of Kansas City, Florida State University and the Stanford campus in Austria.

The following article was published in "Theatre Craft" magazine in January/February, 1968.

Primeval Crystals for "Prometheus Bound"

by Douglas A. Russell

The Stanford Repertory Theatre, with the help of a Rockefeller grant, came into being the autumn of 1965. The University was embarking on a new venture; it had set up the repertory group to merge with the teaching program. It was a promising venture: the group consisted of twelve professional actors, two renowned guest directors, some mature graduate students, and a superior design and technical staff. The only drawback seemed to be the facilities. Built in 1937, Stanford's unwieldy plant offers a 1700-seat theatre and a 200-seat theatre, but nothing in between.

For its inaugural season, the Repertory Theatre chose three plays intended to interest the guest directors, challenge the professional company and present a balanced program to the public. After "Scapin" and "The Skin of Our Teeth" had earned positive reviews, the group relaxed and felt the battle of the first season had been won.

Still "Prometheus Bound," the final production slated for the larger stage, posed formidable challenges. The play requires a chorus of fifteen well-trained women, but the group had only three professional actresses and among the advanced acting students, only three or four girls were available. Our guest director was Eric Vos, on leave from the Neue Komedie in The Hague. To him, the Chorus was the heart and core of the play, and he refused to consider other aspects of our production before it was cast. He scoured the community, even auditioning women who had good voices and movement but no theatrical experience until, finally, he got his fifteen.

Vos then turned to me, the costume designer and to Richard Hay, the stage designer. Since he had directed "Scapin," Richard and I were familiar with Vos' method of attacking the visual side of the production. Vos gives his designers few initial directives: just some very general limitations and a couple of specific ideas. Many conferences and critiques follow, many false starts and stops, so that the final visual concept is a process of slow, thorough evolution.

For "Prometheus" Vos told us he wanted some kind of raked stage, and a thrust that would cover the first ten center rows. Upon the thrust would be a rock that, at its base, would allow enough space to give the Chorus freedom of movement. The costumes would be nothing that could be labeled Greek; nothing, in fact, specifically human. Vos wanted the actors to suggest not human beings, but representatives of the forces of the Universe that man worshipped at the dawn of history.

It was an exciting assignment. How to begin? Where to start looking for source material? How to cover up the human attributes of the actors without obtaining comic results? Obviously, just as Vos had done, I would have to begin with the Chorus. These daughters of the Ocean, who represent the power of the sea, are on stage throughout the play.

Research Method

I went to the library and brought back books showing all aspects of sea life, from seaweed to octopi. My first

Prometheus was chained to the cleft of a y-shaped crystaline rock and surrounded by a chorus of conical, rock-like costumed figures.

tentative sketches looked as if a group of ballet dancers, in full leotards, had become entangled in skeins of seaweed. Vos and I both realized this was too balletic a concept; it was neither monumental nor elemental, and lacked the mysterious, primeval quality of the play. The silhouette of each Chorus member in repose, we gradually decided, must be very solid; conical, like the shape of a rock or a hillock.

Richard Hay, meanwhile, had been struggling with the problem of creating for center stage a truly monumental rock form with a small base. Finally, among the color plates in a book on precious stones, he happened upon a Y-shaped rock with a glowing crystal surface. Here was his solution. The Y-shape could have tremendous height and still assure that Prometheus, chained in its cleft, would not be stationed too far above the Chorus. And most important, its base would occupy a relatively limited amount of stage space.

The book of precious stones now became my source for the Chorus. In a beautiful cross-section of a piece of malachite I found all the blues and greens, and touches of white that are in the sea, when it laps against the rocks. And in the petal-like formation of the malachite I saw the style of the costume materializing: over a basic conical shape I would build the costume, petal by petal.

Many more ideas came from this book as the gorgeous textures and colors of the stones took root in my imagination. Metal and leather seemed key symbols of Hephaestus, God of the Forge, and a perforated piece of natural gold was key to my design: a leather body garment, eaten away to reveal the brilliance of eroded gold. Cold, sharp shards of calcite suggested the armadillo-like uniforms of Strength and Violence, and the texture of the overlapping disks that clothed Hermes. The color of Prometheus' costume came from the vivid black and blood-red explosions in a piece of moss agate; the texture of Io's, from the sharded, raw surfaces of stibnite.

These inspirations, however, did not come to me all at one time; many of the textures and colors I found in the stones did not develop into costumes until a very late date. When it was time to start the shop work on the costumes,

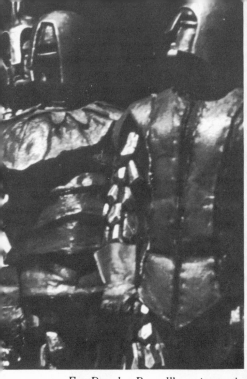

*For Douglas Russell's costumes in
"Prometheus Bound," shards of calcite
inspired the uniforms of Strength and
Violence (above). Io had a pink gown
covered by shredded grassy effects and
melted nylon rock textures (right).*

only the costume for the Chorus had won Vos' approval.

Nonetheless, the Chorus costumes managed to keep the costume shop busy for quite awhile. I had designed the body of the costume in two units: a skirt and a finger-tip cape. This was simple enough for the staff to execute. But I had designated that each section be covered with four dozen, 8-inch by 10-inch petals, and the staff had to do a lot of experimenting with fabrics and plastics to obtain a surface that would combine the right, eroded, rock-like look with the least amount of weight. In the end, the petals were covered with melted nylon that bubbled and eroded into a hard-looking surface. Then they were painted with acrylic pigments until a varicolored, blue-green, rock texture emerged, and tipped with foam white.

We had decided to cover the heads of the Chorus with masks made of fiberglass. Vos, mask-maker Bill Jones, and

203

I pored over books on masks and figurines of Africa and the South Sea Islands, searching for a suitable primitive shape. We finally found it in something that resembled the great heads on Easter Island. It was sad, passive, larger-than-life size; when made up into fiberglass masks, it would be simple and undistracting yet mysterious, indeterminate.

Final Design

What had been holding up the sketches of the other costumes was the problem of establishing, within a unified design framework, a contrast between the forces sympathetic to "Prometheus" and those representing Zeus. We wanted the sympathizers, the earth forces, to project a living, growing organic image. On the other hand, we felt Hermes, Strength, and Violence should look related to the earth, but manufactured and inhuman. And they should have a military, totalitarian quality.

It was this last aspect that troubled us most. How could we indicate militarism without taking the three characters out of the rock-textured world of elemental forces? To us, uniforms of any kind produced worldly, modern connotations. We finally had to compromise and dressed them in weird, over-sized suits of mail. On their legs and arms, they wore overlapping stone shards, manufactured from fiberglass and painted to look sharp, cold, frozen, and dead. Steely breastplates, composed of organically shaped pieces of heavily painted felt, encircled their bodies. Their heads were covered with helmets that almost completely hid the face (a plume of great scaly spines embellished the helmet of Hermes) and their hands were covered with metallic gauntlet gloves.

With the antagonists visually set, we now began to develop Hephaestus, Io, and Oceanus. Hephaestus was the simplest since we already had the image of leather and metal. The eroded gold, which I described earlier, consisted of melted spun glass, painted to look like metal. His helmet-like head piece, also leather and gold, had an earthy, animalistic cast; in fact, his whole silhouette was roughly that of a kindly bear.

Io's costume had not only to suggest her suffering, but her transformation into a cow. We achieved the suffering effect by attaching to a pink gown, shredded grassy effects, melted nylon rock surfaces, and sisal hemp garlands. The pink shone through the exterior texture like raw membranes, and additional membranes, made from transparent nylon webs, decorated her neck and wrists. To symbolize her transformation, we simply designed horns into her sad, tight-featured mask. Then, to symbolize her inability to relate to anyone—to touch another person, either psychologically or physically— we gave her raw pink claws instead of hands.

Prometheus' costume-makeup was inspired by the black-veined, blood red of a moss-agate.

Oceanus, after a period of trial and error, developed into a slightly humorous and pompous figure. He wore a vestment with small rounded stones (styrofoam balls) surrounded by mossy seaweed (sisal hemp), and a mask that crossed a fat, balding man with a walrus. His color scheme was a blue-green, closely allied to the tone of the Chorus.

And finally, we came to Prometheus himself, the one figure who had to suggest both the attributes of a god and a human being. This concept, difficult to establish at best, was complicated by the fact that the actor playing Prometheus was not very large. Vos, therefore, wanted him placed high in the cleft of the rock and the outlines of his human form emphasized. So, seizing my inspiration from the piece of moss agate, I had huge blood-red and black veins drawn over his entire body. Veined, masked, with a great yoke of rock (foam rubber) around his torso, Prometheus looked tortured, but shot through with the strength and power of fire.

Costumes In Use

At last we had a complete cast of characters designed to give a unified visual effect and to integrate with the set. The set was now taking final shape. It was simple and striking: just the great crystalline rock about forty feet high, and some delicately "cut stone" circles which created the raked stage floor. The set extended approximately ten rows out into the auditorium, and the entire production actually took place beyond the proscenium arch.

The first trial run with partially-finished costumes revealed a number of problems. The Chorus' costumes were too heavy and had to be cut down, and their masks needed better ventilation and more cushioning. The overlapping fiberglass shards that Strength, Violence, and Hermes wore on their arms and legs made too much noise; each one had to be backed with felt, and the ones at the top of the inner leg had to be removed. The eye and mouth area of several of the masks needed enlarging; Prometheus found his so distracting that it had to be reduced to the barest minimum.

In later rehearsals there were other technical adjustments to be made. At first trial, the white flicks of foam around the edges of the Chorus costume petals had not "read" from the auditorium, but at the first dress rehearsal, the white edges looked false and much too strong. We finally found the right accent by using a different brush stroke. Again and again, lighting had to be adjusted to suit the costumes. Texture was the central visual effect of the entire production, so we had to be certain that the costumes would read at the right level. The Chorus was very ragged at first, and had to learn how to move within their tent-like vestments in ways that would produce dramatic visual effects.

On opening night, however, the production jelled into an exciting unified ritual, surging and receding about the narrow base of the subtly glowing Y-shaped rock. In describing the visual effects to their readers, the critics flew to metaphorical heights. One saw the Chorus as "weird and barbaric birds who move with a ghostly flutter as they mesmerizingly intone their omniscient dirges." A second saw the Chorus as "primeval nuns in a chapel," and a third, as "robed greenish tiered plumage, much like birds with monkey-like masks." Prometheus was a kind of "Christ on His Cross . . . with his golden, blood-stained limbs writhing in the chains that bind him to that immense rock." Oceanus was a figure rising "from the sea like a massive sea creature, clothed in polished pebbles and dripping seaweed."

The production was a resounding success, praised for its outstanding directing and disciplined choral work, as well as its new visual concept. Vos himself was so pleased with the results that he presented a new production of the play at the Holland Festival last summer. And everyone who worked on Stanford's "Prometheus" considers it to be the repertory theatre's most significant effort to date.

207

Florence Klotz's variations in color and texture to connote different periods of time simultaneously—both the present and time remembered—surely reveal the costume designer's creative contribution at its most subtle and sensitive. Her designs for the Hal Prince Production of "Follies," which opened at the Winter Garden Theatre on April 4, 1971, received as much comment on Broadway as any costume designs in two seasons. In Glenn Loney's article, first published in "Theatre Crafts" in May/June, 1971, designer Klotz makes clear the delicate collaboration between costume designer, set designer, and lighting designer that must exist to achieve the highest level of professionalism and unified refinement.

Among her list of costume credits are the designs for Hal Prince's first movie, "Something for Everybody," and his productions of "Take Her, She's Mine" and "Superman." In addition, her work has been seen in "Never Too Late," "Nobody Loves an Albatross," "The Owl and the Pussycat," "Paris is Out," and "Norman, Is That You?."

Glenn Loney, a contributing editor of "Theatre Crafts" magazine, is a Professor of Theatre at Brooklyn College. He is also on the editorial boards of "Theatre Today" and "Players" and contributes regularly to "Cue," "After Dark," "Opera News," and "Dance Magazine."

Glenn Loney is now at work on two books, "Opera as Theatre" and "Musical Comedy at Home and Abroad."

Florence Klotz's
Recollections for "Follies"

by Glenn M. Loney

When thousands of dollars are involved in a business venture, astute executives do everything they can to plan ahead, to cover their risks, to economize on costs and maximize effects. Oddly enough, in the commercial theatre, such sensible measures are more often the exception than the rule.

But, in a show produced by Hal Prince, very little is left to chance. The collaborators know what they are doing, and they know how to work with each other—many of them having been associated with previous Prince productions.

The themes, the moods, the materials of the musical are thoroughly discussed with all the major artists and technicians quite early in the gestation process. Prince works hard; his associates work hard; and he encourages them to push their creativity to its outer limits, within the general framework of the show's possibilities. When some-

210

thing turns out to be wrong, in terms of all the other elements, of course, it must be changed or discarded. Otherwise a designer has a free hand.

The costume designer for Hal Prince's musical show, "Follies," is Florence Klotz. She recalls, "It was in September 1970 that I had my first conferences with Hal. We talked and talked and talked. Lots of meetings. He told me his interpretation. *What* the show would be about; *who* it would be about; *how* he, as producer-director, sees it. Then I said: 'Go away for a while. Let me see what I can come up

211

with!' At first, he said: 'Let's do it with a Fellini feeling.' So I started out LARGE. Then we came together again to talk about the ideas. We looked at it—it was just *too* large. So we reduced the scale, we came back in again. I've even gone the other way now.

"Of course there were a number of conferences with Boris Aronson, the set designer. One has to know what the director wants, but it's just as important to know what the sets will be like—dimensions, line, color, etc. Lighting is important, too, but that comes after."

Embroidery, beading, sequining, and fabric painting, such as hearts and flowers trimmings (above and below), were some of the handworked details in Florence Klotz's "Follies" costumes.

212

The on-stage environment of "Follies" is the ruins of the Winter Garden Theatre—or what the Winter Garden might look like after the wreckers did to it what they did to Joseph Urban's *chef d'oeuvre*, the Ziegfeld Theatre. What the audience will see on stage—in addition to Alexis Smith, Dorothy Collins, and other luminaries—will be piles of rubble. But, it will be Boris Aronson rubble, which means anything but routine piles of bricks and plaster. Actually, the rubble-heaps will be cleverly constructed ramps and stairs for the performers.

The show was inspired by a James Goldman drama, "The Girls Upstairs." Goldman, who wrote "The Lion in Winter," offers the "Follies" his vision of a reunion in the rubble. (The composer-lyricist is Stephen Sondheim, who did the honors for Prince's "Company.") A party is being given by a former Follies producer, who had invited those who have been close to him—those who worked in his shows. In the course of the party, memories of the past are introduced among those exercising their nostalgia. At the close, in a grand, glorious hallucination, a complete Follies decor comes down out of nowhere into the ruins, and a company of young performers (not previously seen) shows its stuff. Obviously, such novelties of plotting need thorough planning to work on stage. And the role of the costumer is clearly one of the most important in making such devices succeed.

"Follies," obviously, is more than just a nostalgic echo of Florenz Ziegfeld. "There is more of a design problem than just re-creating "Follies" costumes of yesteryear," designer Klotz points out. "The real "Follies"—not those M-G-M film versions—were never as flashy as most people think. And I have to design for real character people in "Follies," as well as for all the young characters and the singing-and-dancing people. There are about 52 actors. Some of them have a number of changes. So there are about 120 costumes which had to be designed and built. That, in itself, is about average for a musical. But, there is a lot of work in each costume.

"The older people are not doing an onstage fashion show! They and their costumes mean something. Some come from the Midwest. Some come from down South. They have character and personality. My costumes have to help express those qualities. When you do a Fifi D'Orsay, you put her in lots of feathers, and sequins, and bows! I mean: that's Fifi! Then you get a lady with nine children, who comes from a small town somewhere – she's in a drab outfit.

"When the actors first came for fittings, some asked me, 'What period are you doing "Follies" in?' And I said, 'Every period, because you're not rich. You're an old Ziegfeld Girl. You haven't been to a party in a LONG time. But you've still got a closet full of lovely clothes from the old days. Perfectly good, marvelously cut, wonderful fabrics – but they're all twenty, thirty, forty years old!'"

"You mean," "Theatre Crafts" asked, "they're supposed to be thinking: There's lots of wear in that gown yet, and I used to look so beautiful in it – never mind that it's a little out of-style?"

"Yes," Miss Klotz replied, "or they can be thinking about making up a crazy costume, or wearing some stage get-up from one of their big numbers – something they hauled out of a trunk. Alexis Smith and her husband are the only really rich people in the show – the two of them will be like a king and queen. Dorothy Collins is a funny lady who is supposed to have made her own dress for this party. It's a little bouffant, but you don't notice that so much. She told me that the last time she wore something like it was on the "Hit Parade." In this show, the actors understand what they are doing, and why they are dressed the way they are.

214

Down Memory Lane

"This show is so very exciting – a tremendous undertaking! If the theatre doesn't dig this, then I really don't know where we can go from here. Wonderful as Boris Aronson's setting of theatre rubble is, the costumes do have to bring color to the stage. You don't want your audience to be depressed. There is a Memory number – the memories of the central characters in the musical – themselves when they were young, their visions of the past. The party people – the character roles – are all in low-key colors. Because in all my memories people are in black and white. So I couldn't put the older men at the party in black

Rather frumpy and over stated feathers and spangles
bedeck a former Follies girl (played by Fifi D'Orsay) as
she recollects the dim memory of herself as a young
showgirl. Florence Klotz's costume and sketch for that
earlier vision show a sleek chic embroidered satin culotte
sheath with a bespangled tiara of white peacock feathers.

In a rectangle-patched floor-length cloak of satin and velvet (right), ex-Follies girl Phyllis (played by Alexis Smith) conjures up a memory of her younger more exposed days in feathers and diamond-shaped patches embroidered with pearls.

216

evening dress. Instead, the leading man is in an eggplant or aubergine color. It is going to be *the* color for men's wear this season. I didn't know that before, when I chose it; it was just a lucky guess.

"Also, I had to find a solution for the memory costumes that would keep them from being drab or ghostlike. Even though they are in black and white, there is going to be a *slight* color accent in it. Maybe nobody but me and the costume builders will know about it, but it will be there. It won't register strongly. I don't want it to. What is the secret color? Well, it's not so much of a color, as a variation of shading. You'll be seeing dark and light whites and blacks. But you won't know *why* — if you are aware of them at all. I have to do this or the costumes would be flat. For that reason, I'm using wool and cotton fabrics which will look different under the lights.

A dancing couple at the Follies reunion pairs with the recollection of the figure they cut in younger more dashing days.

217

"Another important aspect of this scene is that the costume materials are all ALIVE. When I say 'Alive' I mean materials which reflect light rather than absorb it. I've used satins which reflect, crushed velvets which reflect, and lots of beads and sequins—they positively glitter. All the laces and nets on my brides' costumes are embroidered with sequins to pick up the light. The sequins are done by hand. It is expensive but the beading and sequining is all being done at Matera's studio, as are all the women's clothes, so we are able to control the work. Also the men's clothes for the final "Follies" number. Usually such delicate work is sent out, but this is so special it needs to be watched and guided.

"What's the secret about the final "Follies" sequence?" "Theatre Crafts" inquired. "It is supposed to be a hallucination—but what kind of hallucination? Back to Joseph Urban and Erté, or forward to Bill Graham and Peter Max?"

"Boris Aronson and I started with Erté," said Miss Klotz. "I did it first—and then this new, lovely book on Erte came out, after. Boris and I were talking in the planning stage—we knew we were expected to design a final "Follies"' number—and he asked me: 'Why can't we do columns, columns, columns?' So I went to the Metropolitan Museum's costume collection. I looked up design of old "Follies" costumers. I even went to the Ziegfeld Girls' Club—yes they still have a club here! I did research like crazy. And I did the final number all in the style of Erté.

"Then Steve Sondheim wrote a new final number, 'Loveland.' I saw it, and instantly thought of Dresden china figurines. Ziegfeld often had period costume numbers and that was it. They liked it. Back to the drawing board I went. The Dresden Doll idea is right. It's all in pale colors, ice-cream colors, valentine colors, cotton candy colors. An entirely different trip than an Erté hallucination would have been!"

Costumes and Lighting

"Naturally I have worked very closely on "Follies" with lighting designer Tharon Musser as well as with set designer Boris Aronson. For Tharon, I make a whole costume-chart and plot. The chart deals with costumes, colors, fabrics. The plot is a detailed outline of how and when the costumes appear on stage (this couple is coming on at this point in the book, from this side; these people will be grouped over here, down stage left). Tharon comes up here to the studio and studies my sketches. She analyzes the fabrics and the colors carefully; she studies the over-all color schemes to be sure her lighting will work with the materials and hues."

That is something that many members of the theatre audience may not have realized. Not to mention costumers of community theatre and some college productions, who are appalled to see their lovely costumes appear to change color and quality once stage-light is thrown on them. It is, of course, the business of professional costumers and lighting-designers to know about the tricks which will make costumes and material look better—as well as about the dangers—those conjunctions of fabric, color, and light which will destroy the desired effect.

"Yes," designer Florence Klotz goes on to point out, "a bastard amber, a surprise pink can work quite differently on different materials, even though the color of the various materials seems to be the same. That may have to do with the chemical composition of the dyes, the density of the material, the kind of weave, the sort of fibre—cotton, wool, synthetic. It is our job to know that, or find it out. You know that colors and fabrics look different under flourescent light, lamplight, sunlight, and stage-light. They look different under a bright, white spot-light than they do under conventional stage lighting."

219

As an example of how she and Tharon Musser are using lighting to their advantage, designer Klotz explains that the shadings in the black and white memory sequence achieved by using wool and cotton fabrics are because "white wool gives a yellow-white under light. White cotton gives a white-white. Under Tharon's stage lights—as she agrees—they'll look more or less alike, at first. But, when one of the Memory characters comes into the spot-light, the difference will be visible—subtle, but visible."

"Theatre Crafts" asked if it happens now and again that a fabric which would be just fine, exactly right for a certain costume cannot be used because the way it takes light throws it out of balance with the other costumes on stage?

"Of course!" Designer Klotz answered, "That's why Tharon is here during the early stages of costume design and construction. She is controlling this, and it saves a lot of trouble later, when we might have to use other materials, colors, or even a whole costume—not to mention changing the lighting as well.

"Of course something can go wrong with a costume when you see it on stage for the first time in rehearsal— something you won't be able to realize until you see the costume being used. But, that doesn't mean the number itself has to be discarded or redone. If the premise of the routine is sound, then it's the costume that has to be changed—not the number. Let me explain it this way: when I design, I make all the sketches; then, I put all the colors down, as in a painting. Now, if you take one of those colors away from me, I've lost a bit of that painting. That color is important to me. It may not matter to a director. He may not even notice if it's omitted. But to me it's a value I need very much in my total design-color concept. But, I'm still talking about all this *on paper*, in the design and construction stage. I don't know what's going to happen, really, until the costumes get on stage, and all of the people wearing them become live. Then I can say, 'Oh boy! How did that yellow get in there?'"

"What do you do when the costumes get on stage and you discover that colors are focusing attention in the wrong place?" "Theatre Crafts" inquired.

"When a director is looking at the composition—or a choreographer is setting a dance number," Designer Klotz replied, "they will usually notice such things at once. *Somebody* will! Then things will be sorted out, re-arranged. The choreographer can help immensely by re-arranging the dancers. That way, not only do costumes not have to be discarded nor new ones made, but an especially interesting costume—which no one really thought was at all interesting until they saw it under light—can be brought forward where it can be seen."

Florence Klotz's notebook for "Follies" is full of elaborate, Erté-esque costume sketches like those for showgirls (above and below) and for a bride (left).

Working Methods

Florence Klotz is surrounded by fabric samples and assistants rushing in and out. On the floor below, the costumes are being built. On designer Klotz's bulletin board is a snapshot of a plump lady of a somewhat faded loveliness. A Ziegfeld Girl! Florence Klotz and her cohorts had been invited to a Ziegfeld Girl party, and it was just as she had envisioned it. Her party costumes for the has-beens and forgottens had already been designed. There were the real articles in their old finery!

Costume designer Klotz leafs through a hefty blue 3-ring binder, page after page, all sturdy yellow sheets of costume designs. It is her "bible." On the left-hand page are all the swatches of material used in the costume, together with any special decorations. One of them has an ermine tail, and just under it, a fall of black, white, and clear glass beads, which will glitter briefly every time the wearer of the costume moves. On the right-hand page is a sharp xerox copy of one of the many dazzling designs. On one page, there are four different kinds of machine lace — the patterns and sizes of pattern differ. Why so many?

"What I've done with many costumes, to achieve the special effects I want under light, is to put material on top of material on top of material. Sometimes as many as five layers. And the embroidery — all done by hand — the beading, the sequins, the feathers — all tied by hand. And some of the fabric has been hand-painted — especially in the Dresden Doll number, in which the costumes have marvelous flowers, also hand-made. This is a lot of work — but it is worth it. Delicate as they may seem, these costumes are built to hold up! We have an excellent wardrobe mistress who knows how to take care of them. During the days she will be at the theatre sewing, stitching, pressing. If there is a major repair or alteration, she can take the costume over to Matera's.

"I will go with the show on out-of-town tryout to Boston. My two assistants, some people from Matera's, some fabric-painters, and a tailor will go, too. (I never do any actual sewing myself.) There are always last minute changes. The other day, Dorothy Collins needed a new costume for the "Follies" number. What to do? What about

222

Jean Harlow style? Hal Prince said: 'Marvelous!' I gave him a finished sketch on Sunday. Today, Monday one day later, it's being built. Next Monday it's being shipped to Boston.

"Of course this show has been a challenge. Although 120 costumes is about the average number for a Broadway musical, the way they are being made takes as much work as twenty-five costumes. Of course, it is costing a lot—though not nearly as much as it might have. I hope the show looks like a million!"

Photo Credits:

pp. 40, 44 top: Fletcher Drake

p. 44 bottom: George de Vincent

pp. 46, 47: Ronald L. Freeman

pp. 50, 51 top: Fletcher Drake

p. 51 bottom: Ronald L. Freeman

p. 52: Fletcher Drake

p. 77 bottom: Stan Enstrom

pp. 78, 80 bottom, 81, 83: Courtesy, Illinois Institute of Technology and the Art Gallery of Toronto

p. 80 top: Courtesy, Weslyan University Press (Middletown, Conn.) from *The Theatre of the Bauhaus.*

p. 86: Susan Schiff-Faludi

pp. 87, 88, 89, 90 bottom: David Berlin

p. 90 top: Brynn Manley

p. 93: Susan Schiff-Faludi

p. 95 top, bottom right: David Berlin

p. 97: Susan Schiff-Faludi

p. 102 top, 104 top: Eric Sutherland

p. 105: Zodiac

p. 157: Lee Owens and Patrick Owens

p. 172: John Veltri

pp. 210, 211, 215 top: Martha Swope

p. 215 bottom left: Zodiac

pp. 216, 217: Martha Swope

Art Direction: Charles F. Beck